The SAN DIEGO BREWERY GUIDE

Published by Georgian Bay Books, Inc. (an imprint of Georgian Bay, LLC)
San Diego, California
www.georgianbaybooks.com

Publisher & President: Bruce Glassman

Text: Bruce Glassman
Photographs: Mike Pawlenty and Bruce Glassman
Cover Design: Amy Stirnkorb
Copyeditor: Jessica Knott
Interior Design and Proofreading: berniergraphics.com

How to use this guide:

 Highly Recommended  Recommended

   Denotes location as one of three sectors of San Diego County, used for reference with maps beginning on page 144.

Percentages under beer names: ABV (alcohol by volume)

Special thanks to: Mel Daversa, Sabrina LoPiccolo, and Amber Crocker for all their help in coordinating. Extra-special thanks to Candice Eley from the San Diego Tourism Authority for her invaluable help in pulling this project together.

And thanks to: Tom Burnett, Dave Busse, and especially Jim Crute, who were essential partners in tasting and evaluating all these beers . . .

ISBN: 978-0-9896142-1-4

First Edition
Printed in the USA

The SAN DIEGO BREWERY GUIDE

Essential trip-planning advice, at-a-glance facts, and tasting notes on every brewery from A–Z

BRUCE GLASSMAN

georgianbay books

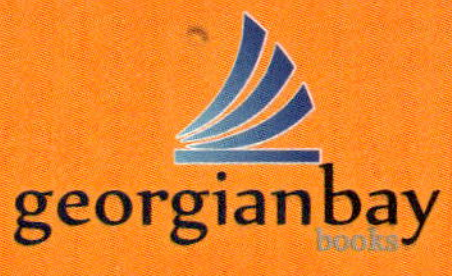

San Diego, California

INSIDE

FOREWORD from Joe Terzi

RECENTLY, I HAD THE HONOR of joining some of San Diego's top brewers at a San Diego State University alumni event focused on the business of craft beer. Sitting amongst these beer experts and listening to them share their incredible knowledge of the industry, it was clear that I was the beer rookie of the group. I may still be learning about the difference between an IPA and an Imperial IPA, but there's one thing I do know: there is no better destination in the U.S. for enjoying craft beer than San Diego.

When I began my tenure as the President & CEO of the San Diego Tourism Authority in 2008, there were just over 20 breweries in San Diego. Today, the region boasts nearly 80, with more slated to open in the coming year. But the craft beer boom hasn't been contained to San Diego. Between 2007 and 2012, sales of craft beer in the U.S. nearly doubled, and while the rest of the nation's thirst for craft beer grew, San Diego stepped into the spotlight. It wasn't long before leading media outlets including *Men's Journal*, *The New York Times*, and CNN were singing the praises of San Diego as the country's top craft beer destination.

Of course, with the astounding growth we've seen over the years, many visitors have asked me, "Why has craft beer flourished in San Diego?" To many who live here, craft beer epitomizes the San Diego lifestyle: first-class, yet laid-back. San Diego defines itself as a destination with all the vibrancy of a big city without any of the attitude, and our craft breweries reflect just that. While many of them are producing award-winning brews, they welcome you with a warm smile and friendly greeting when you step up to the bar for a pint. It's this welcoming spirit that makes the San Diego craft beer experience rewarding for even the most novice beer enthusiast.

Brewery tourism is an important part of San Diego's tourism offerings. Much like our weather, our breweries welcome visitors year-round. For years, people have known about our beautiful beaches and world-class family attractions, and now San Diego's craft beer scene offers visitors the chance to experience a side of San Diego that many out-of-towners haven't seen before.

Joe Terzi

And it's not just visitors to San Diego that benefit from a refreshing pint of ale. According to a recent study by National University, San Diego's craft beer industry generated $300 million in economic impact for the local community in 2011; the industry also created or sustained about 3,000 jobs during this same time period. Of course, tourism is one of the biggest economic drivers in San Diego. It is the second-largest traded economy in the city, generating $18.3 billion in economic impact and employing 160,000 San Diegans. Both craft beer and tourism are vital to San Diego's economic future, and together, we can make a bigger impact than we ever could alone.

So come visit San Diego, and use this guide to get to know our incredible brewers and the terrific beers they make. Not only will you be enjoying world-class beer in America's Finest City, but you'll also be joining an earnest community of locals ready to welcome you to the fold—that's something worth toasting.

Joe Terzi
President & CEO
San Diego Tourism Authority

PREFACE from Bruce Glassman

FIVE YEARS AGO, A BOOK LIKE THIS would not have been possible. Back then, San Diego only had about twenty-something breweries that were actual, going concerns, making enough beer to sell to the public. Today, San Diego County has nearly 80 working breweries, with an estimated 20 to 25 more in the planning stages. The number of breweries has more than doubled in the past two years. The growth is mind-boggling.

This project was, in large part, inspired by our best brewers. They are the men and women who deserve to be called out and acknowledged in a guide such as this. With 75+ breweries to choose from, the task of figuring out where to start and where to visit is not easy—and it's growing more complex by the day. For one thing, the sheer growth in numbers makes it inevitable that not every brewery in San Diego is doing gold-medal beer. In addition, every brewery has its own particular focus and beer-style preferences. Given all the variables, our goal is to help you understand the playing field—both geographically and quality-wise—and to help you navigate the many choices you'll have to make as you plan your visits.

The SAN DIEGO BREWERY GUIDE is meant to help you sort out, at a glance, where to start and how you want to spend your time. The best way to show you how to spend your time is to tell you what we consider to be the best breweries. Our rating system is very basic—we have broken every brewery into one of three categories: Highly Recommended (⁚), Recommended (•), and Everybody Else. We wanted to approach our ratings in a way that, at one end, would highlight what we consider the best, but at the other end would not necessitate being actively negative. So the ⁚ and • designations are beers and breweries we feel clearly stand out in the crowd. Those without one of those designations, we feel, may make perfectly fine beer but do not merit your first consideration or special attention. We are not implying that these beers or breweries are "not recommended," but rather simply that—if you have to make a choice—you should focus your initial time and efforts on the more exceptional producers.

Keep in mind, also, that the tasting notes and recommendations are based on the specific palates of a small group of people. These people are experts with

Bruce Glassman

lots of beer-tasting experience, but they are nonetheless just individuals with individual preferences and tastes. So, the tasting notes are meant to be a jumping-off point for you to consider what you smell and taste, and for you to decide whether or not you like what you taste. You may disagree with our notes. They may not match what you experience. No matter what the outcome, if you're tasting the beer with intention—paying attention and making your own sensory notes—you're going to get something valuable from the experience.

In addition to beer-tasting notes, we have included basic information on what you can expect when you get to each tasting room. The intention is to offer the kinds of details you might want to know ahead of time if you were traveling with friends or family. Is the location kid-friendly? Is there a place for dogs? Is there a place for grandma to sit down once we're there? Is food available? Do they do tours? Can we fill growlers? Buy bottles?

While doing the research for this book as well as two other beer books over the course of the past five years, I've gotten to know San Diego's brewers very well. And I've gotten a unique opportunity to taste most of the beers they make. (I tasted about 600 beers for this book alone!) I can wholeheartedly say that San Diego brewers are a great bunch. Ask any San Diego brewer and they'll tell you that the brewing community is guided by a truly exceptional sense of camaraderie. It's a community that the brewers feel privileged to be part of—and it's a community you'll feel proud to support. And, lucky for us, there's one exceptionally fun and tasty way to go and show them your support. So get out there! And enjoy!

INTRODUCTION from Peter Rowe

THE ALE WAS STRONG, DARK, CONFIDENT to the point of—as the label warned—arrogance.

Yes, Stone's Arrogant Bastard Ale has a definite personality.

In nearly 20 years of writing about beer, I've encountered ales and lagers of nearly every description. Some are buttoned-down, corporate types, with all quirks or distinguishing characteristics scrubbed off, as if they had been designed by a committee.

But the best beers are as unique as the best people. Meeting them is a special, one-of-a-kind experience, whether they are saucy gingers (Green Flash's Hop Head Red), sunny and straightforward blondes (AleSmith's X) or earthy and contemplative sorts who sport a Flemish accent (The Lost Abbey's Lost and Found).

The best way to meet these beers is to sip them. But to truly know these creations, there's no substitute for traveling to their birthplaces and meeting their creators.

As Bruce Glassman shows in this wonderful book, touring all of San Diego County's breweries is a massive job. Our local breweries are spread across one of the United States' largest and most diverse counties, a land of seashores, mountains, and desert. The region is home to so many professional brewers, you'd be hard-pressed to meet all of them in a year. (Especially if some of your time is required by more mundane pastimes—work, say.)

But this is a happy task, and not only because every brewery is well-stocked with liquid refreshment. Perhaps for obvious reasons, brewers are some of the most sociable people on earth. They are wonderful conversationalists with a surprising variety of interests. I've met brewers who are well-versed in medieval history, surfing, the workings of Wall Street the best ramen shops in Osaka, and the dangers of gingivitis.

So it's no wonder that these brewers' products are unique. When these well-rounded individuals focus on brewing beer, that one task is informed by all they've learned and experienced.

Peter Rowe

It's often said that brewing is an art as well as a science. If you are lucky enough to find the right guide—and since you are holding Glassman's book, consider yourself among the fortunate—you will learn that beer is also something else: a story, told in malts, hops, yeast, and water.

These tales are bitter and sweet, familiar and challenging, cheerful and full of unexpected depth. Every pint tells a story. And there's no better way to understand these stories than by sitting down with a brewer in the place where these tales were born.

Let Glassman show you the path. Beer—and enchantment—await.

Peter Rowe, San Diego, August 2013

Peter Rowe is a staff writer for the U-T San Diego and has written about beer since 1995. You can follow his beer bulletins, ale announcements, and hop headlines at facebook.com/#!/BreweryRowe.

ALESHMITH BREWING COMPANY (Miramar)

alesmith.com
9368 Cabot Dr.
San Diego, CA 92126
(858) 549-9888
Mon: Closed
Tue–Thur: 2 pm–8 pm
Fri: 2 pm–9 pm
Sat: 11 am–8 pm
Sun: 11 am–6 pm

ALESMITH IS PART OF WHAT IS CONSIDERED the "first wave" of great San Diego breweries: roughly defined as places that opened their doors between 1989 and 2002. The first AleSmith beer was poured in 1995, and their reputation grew quickly. Since then, the brewery has won major medals in a wide variety of California competitions, as well as national and international festivals, including The Great American Beer Festival and World Beer Cup. Today, the 11,000-square-foot brewery is producing about 12,000 barrels (372,000 gallons) of beer every year.

tasting room	yes
beers on tap	12+
cask / nitro	yes
tours	saturdays
kegs	5 & 15.5 gal.
growlers	32 & 64 oz.
bottles	22 oz. & 750 ml.
six packs	four packs
merchandise	yes
kid friendly	no
dog friendly	yes
seating	no
food	weekend food truck

BEER	COLOR	AROMA	TASTE
horny devil 10% (Belgian strong ale)	light yellow, straw	Belgian yeastiness, coriander, citrus	bright citrus hops, coriander, light bready malt
IPA 7.25%	medium golden, straw	malty with floral and citrus hop notes	hoppy, balanced by rich caramel maltiness, finishes dry
old numbskull 11% (barleywine)	deep caramel	big, rich malt, caramel, toffee	caramel, butterscotch, toffee maltiness balanced by crisp hops
nut brown 5.0%	dark brown	rich malt, hints of nuts	rich malt and chocolate, medium mouthfeel and balanced finish
speedway stout 12%	deep black	roasted coffee, chocolate, toasted caramel	toasted and roasted caramel maltiness with espresso, balanced by crisp bitter hops

• tasters, half pints, pints, and flights available

THEIR COMFORTABLE TASTING ROOM has recently been remodeled, with ample space to stand at a long, beautiful bar or at numerous bar tables and tables made from beer barrels. The vibe at AleSmith is welcoming and friendly, and the service is always excellent.

Under the expert guidance of master brewers Peter Zien and Tod Fitzsimmons, AleSmith focuses primarily on beer styles from Belgium, England, and the United States. You can find a range of brews that go from a lightly hopped extra pale ale, to an IPA, to amber, malty, caramel beers, on up to dark, rich, and robustly flavored. Seasonal beers are often on tap, as is a regular cask selection. All AleSmith's beers are of the highest quality, but don't visit without tasting Old Numbskull (barleywine), Wee Heavy (Scotch Ale), and the highly coveted Speedway Stout.

ALPINE BEER COMPANY (Alpine)

alpinebeerco.com
2351 Alpine Blvd.
Alpine, CA 91901
(619) 445-2337
Sun, Mon: Closed
Tue–Sat: 12 pm–6 pm
Pub Hours:
Tue–Thur: 11 am–10 pm
Fri, Sat: 11 am–Midnight
Sun: 12: pm–9 pm

2

EVEN THOUGH IT IS RELATIVELY SMALL, Alpine Beer Company is one of San Diego's craft beer cornerstones. First opened in 2002, the brewery expanded in 2008 and added a pub next door in 2010.

Located 20 to 30 minutes east of downtown San Diego, Alpine is a destination brewery that is well worth the trip. The small tasting room is primarily for tasters and growler fills, while the cozy pub offers seating, a full menu, and pints of Alpine's beers.

tasting room	yes
beers on tap	10
cask / nitro	yes
tours	no
kegs	no
growlers	64 oz.
bottles	22 oz.
six packs	no
merchandise	yes
kid friendly	no
dog friendly	no
seating	no
food	pub next door

BEER	COLOR	AROMA	TASTE
alpine ale 5.5%	medium golden yellow	bready, malty, yeasty	malty with notes of warm bread; crisp and hoppy with a light mouthfeel
McIlhenney's Irish red 6%	golden amber	caramel, toffee, hints of chocolate	caramel and toffee maltiness with hints of coffee; crisp with a light mouthfeel and slightly sweet finish
duet IPA 7%	medium golden yellow	deep lemon and citrus hops	big lemon, citrus, with notes of honey; medium mouthfeel with crisp, slightly bitter finish
nelson rye IPA 7%	medium-light golden yellow	floral, citrus, hints of white wine	citrus, lemon, bready yeastiness with medium mouthfeel; finishes bitter with slight sweetness
pure hoppiness 8%	medium deep golden	big hops; citrus, grapefruit, honey, floral	big citrus, lemon, grass with medium mouthfeel and crisp, medium-bitter finish

• tasters, pints, and flights available

FATHER-AND-SON TEAM PAT AND SHAWN MCILHENNEY brew the popular Alpine lineup, which includes full-flavored ales, lagers, and sours. Demand often outstrips supply and bottle availability is quite limited, so dedicated hop-heads (who lust after Alpine's great IPAs) will often make the trip just to purchase up to four 22-oz. bottles right at the brewery.

AMPLIFIED ALE WORKS (Pacific Beach)

amplifiedales.com

2

4150 Mission Blvd.
#208
San Diego, CA 92109
(858) 270-5222

Sun–Wed: 11 am–11 pm
Thur–Sat: 11 am–11:30 pm

IN AUGUST 2012, THE OWNERS OF California Kebab House in Pacific Beach started pouring their own house-brewed beers. Perched on the second level of a small mall on Mission Boulevard, the bar and restaurant provides a partial view of the ocean and offers both indoor and outdoor patio seating.

Being only a few thousand feet from the beach, the atmosphere at the Kebab House is naturally hip-casual and laid-back. A small, surfer-inspired dining area opens out onto a medium-sized patio where patrons can sit and sip as they enjoy the ocean breezes.

tasting room	bar / restaurant
beers on tap	5 house / 20 guest
cask / nitro	yes
tours	no
kegs	no
growlers	64 oz.
bottles	no
six packs	no
merchandise	yes
kid friendly	yes
dog friendly	outside patio
seating	good
food	full menu

BEER	COLOR	AROMA	TASTE	
amplified harmonic saison 5%	light yellow	bready, yeasty esters with citrus notes	citrus, bread, crisp with a medium mouthfeel	●
bier de garde 7.7%	medium amber orange	tropical fruit, bubble gum, malty esters	tropical fruit, raisin, grains of paradise, bready with medium-rich mouthfeel and bitter finish	●●

• tasters, pints, 32 oz. mugs, and flights available

AMPLIFIED BREWER CY HENLEY works on a very small system (3-barrel) and, during our visit, only two beers were available for tasting. As production ramps up, the lineup will include a variety of styles, such as a Belgian quad, a stout, and various IPAs. If the saison and bier de garde are any indication, the quality of Amplified's production should be quite good.

AUTOMATIC BREWING COMPANY (Normal Heights)

automaticbrewingco.com

3

3416 Adams Ave.
San Diego, CA 92116
(619) 255-2491

Mon: Closed; Tue–Sun: 11:30 am–11:59 pm

HOUSED INSIDE BLIND LADY ALE HOUSE, Automatic Brewing is the nano-brewing side of the operation. Lee Chase, former brewer at Stone and one of the four partners in Blind Lady, has developed some space within the ale house to do some of his own brewing. The brew operation is small, kind of hidden, and not operating on a set schedule. But the production is well worth seeking out.

Blind Lady is a comfortable and welcoming place, and it's popular with locals as well as craft beer insiders. Long, communal-style wooden tables provide ample seating and create a warm, social atmosphere that's particularly family

tasting room	bar / tavern
beers on tap	26+
cask / nitro	yes
tours	no
kegs	no
growlers	yes
bottles	no
six packs	no
merchandise	yes
kid friendly	yes
dog friendly	no
seating	large
food	yes

BEER	COLOR	AROMA	TASTE
automatic pilot pale 5.7%	medium golden straw	light malt, floral hops	medium hoppy with a touch of sweet honey and medium bitterness
nitro coffee stout 5.5%	deep brown	roasty coffee and chocolate	malt forward, chocolate, coffee with a rich creamy head
circa stout 5.5%	dark brown	malty chocolate	rich, malty with chocolate notes

• tasters, half pints, pints, pitchers, and flights available

friendly. The kitchen provides a nice selection of simple un-fussy food and includes organic and vegan options along with house-made chorizo, salami, and other carnivore's delights.

WITH 26 TAPS, BLIND LADY OFFERS a fine selection of great craft beer that always includes admirable representation from San Diego and usually includes at least a few Automatic Brewing options. Their sister establishment—Tiger! Tiger!—is located only about a mile away on El Cajon Boulevard. There is no on-site brewing there, but the friendly vibe and approach are similar.

AZTEC / 7 NATIONS BREWING COMPANY (Vista)

aztecbrewery.com
2330 La Mirada Dr.
#300
Vista, CA 92081
(760) 598-7720
Mon–Wed: Closed
Thur, Fri: 4 pm–9 pm
Sat: 12 pm–7 pm
Sun: 12 pm–5 pm

STEADY GROWTH IN SIZE AND POPULARITY has characterized Aztec's foray into the craft beer business. Opened in 2011, on the heels of a few other Vista-based operations, co-founders John Webster, Claudia Faulk, and Rob Esposito were determined to distinguish Aztec with a strong brand and a variety of beers that offered unique attributes within their respective styles.

The recently expanded tasting room is comfortable and roomy enough, with good seating options and a small bar. Natural light can be something of a challenge, though this is helped when the garage door is rolled up.

tasting room	yes
beers on tap	9
cask / nitro	no
tours	by request
kegs	5 & 15.5 gal.
growlers	64 oz.
bottles	22 oz.
six packs	no
merchandise	yes
kid friendly	yes
dog friendly	yes
seating	good
food	thur–sat food truck

BEER	COLOR	AROMA	TASTE
hibiscus wheat 4.5%	medium golden yellow	light maltiness mixed with floral tropical fruit notes	sweet honey and hibiscus with notes of allspice and cardamom
agave wheat 5.1%	hazy deep golden yellow	fruity esters, sweet honey, honeysuckle	banana, warm bread, tropical fruit with a clean crisp finish
aztec amber ale 5.7%	deep orange	malty caramel and toffee with hint of hops	toffee malt, crisp and balanced; finishes slightly sweet
chipotle IPA 6.6%	medium orange	sweet honey and bready malt, light hop aroma	crisp citrus hops followed by a hint of smoky spice; finishes slightly sweet with trailing bitterness
sacrifice red IPA 7.6%	deep copper red	rich malty caramel and toffee	malty caramel up front, followed by crisp, bright ctirus hops; a touch of sweetness balanced by bitterness

• tasters, half pints, pints, and flights available

AZTEC'S NEW BREWER, PAUL NAYLOR, offers a range of beers to fit almost any palate, from light Kolsch-styles to malty-hoppy reds, to IPAs, all the way through stouts and spiced beers. A recent focus has been on creating full-flavored beers with lower ABVs so the brewery can offer a larger range of truly sessionable brews.

BACK STREET BREWERY (Vista)

lamppostpizza.com

1

15 Main St.
Vista, CA 92083
(760) 407-7600

Sun–Thur: 11 am–11 pm
Fri: 11 am–12 am
Sat: 11 am–12 am

THIS FAMILY-FRIENDLY BREWPUB and pizza restaurant, located on Main Street in downtown Vista, is a long-standing member of the booming craft beer community in San Diego's North County.

Back Street offers a nice range of seating and sipping options for visitors. In addition to the big bar and bar tables in the brewery area, there is also a large outdoor patio and a large pizza restaurant adjacent to the space. A wide selection of pizzas, salads, sandwiches, and pasta dishes are available no matter where you sit.

tasting room	bar / restaurant
beers on tap	8 house / 8 guest
cask / nitro	cask
tours	no
kegs	no
growlers	64 oz.
bottles	no
six packs	no
merchandise	yes
kid friendly	yes
dog friendly	yes
seating	very good
food	full menu

BEER	COLOR	AROMA	TASTE	
jagged little pilsner 4.3%	light yellow	light European malt	light maltiness, crisp and clean	
heritage hef 5.5%	hazy golden yellow	bready esters with clove and grapefruit	clove, bready, with notes of pepper; crisp	●●
alf's amber ale 5.5%	copper amber	caramel, toffee	caramel and toffee with notes of warm bread; light mouthfeel, crisp with slightly sweet finish	●
rydin' dirty IPA 7.2%	golden yellow	big lemon, citrus, and honey hops	big citrus, lemon, and grapefruit, with medium mouthfeel, good bitterness and slightly sweet finish	●●

- tasters, half pints, pints, 32 oz. mugs, pitchers, and flights available

BREWER CHRIS GORT supplies the bar, pub, and pizzeria with its tasty house beers. He brews a modest ale-centric lineup of accessible beers that go well with food, and he always features a nice selection of sessionable beers that don't knock you out after one pint.

BALLAST POINT BREWING & SPIRITS (Scripps Ranch)

ballastpoint.com

10051 Old Grove Rd.
San Diego, CA 92131

(858) 695-2739

Mon–Sat: 11 am–9 pm
Sun 12 pm–7 pm

2

BALLAST POINT IS ONE OF THE BREWERIES that played a major role in focusing the world's craft beer spotlight on San Diego. The production brewery has been growing and producing great beers since 1996, but it wasn't until they became the 2010 World Beer Cup Champion Brewery (voted the best small brewery in the world) that their growth became truly explosive.

Increased fame has recently required the brewery to triple its tasting room space by busting down numerous walls and creating an outdoor patio area with plenty of tables and seating. Bar tables and a nice long bar inside also offer ample surfaces to rest your elbows and your pints.

tasting room	yes
beers on tap	20+
cask / nitro	yes
tours	every day - 12, 2, 4, 6
kegs	5 & 15.5 gal.
growlers	64 & 128 oz.
bottles	12 & 22 oz.
six packs	bottles & cans
merchandise	yes
kid friendly	yes
dog friendly	outside patio
seating	good
food	tue–sun food truck

BEER	COLOR	AROMA	TASTE
pale ale 5.2%	golden yellow	biscuit, bready yeasts with fruity notes	light maltiness balanced by crisp fruity hops
calico amber ale 5.5%	deep amber copper	caramel and toffee with hints of dry fruit	caramel, toffee with hints of raisins balanced by a crisp, bitter finish
sculpin IPA 7%	deep golden orange	grapefruit, lemon, mango, peach	mango, grapefruit, lemon with notes of black pepper and spices; medium mouthfeel with a crisp bitter finish
black marlin porter 6%	deep dark brown	chocolate and roasted coffee with hints of vanilla	chocolate, caramel, coffee balanced by a crisp hop acidity with a slightly sweet finish

• tasters, half pints, pints, and flights available

ALTHOUGH THEY ARE PERHAPS MOST FAMOUS for their award-winning Sculpin IPA, this is a brewery that produces almost every style of beer, and—thanks in large part to the impressive talents of Yuseff Cherney—does everything well. In addition to their breadth and depth, Ballast Point is also an innovator. Chile beers, coffee beers, and sours and saisons flavored with local ingredients are just a few of the items you're likely to find on tap during any given week. If you're lucky enough to happen in to the tasting room while some form of Indra Kunindra or Victory at Sea are available, don't miss them.

BALLAST POINT / HOME BREW MART (Linda Vista)

ballastpoint.com

2

5401 Linda Vista Rd.
San Diego, CA 92110
(619) 295-2337

Mon–Fri: 11 am–7 pm
Sat: 9 am–7 pm
Sun: 10 am–5 pm

STEPPING INTO HOME BREW MART is like stepping into a monument to San Diego Craft Beer. For a vast array of pro brewers in town, this is the place where it all began. In fact, HBM's recently retired brewhouse has been placed on exhibit at the San Diego History Center.

Home Brew Mart is, first and foremost, a homebrew supply store with a brewing facility in back. It does happen to have, however, some of the best and most interesting beer in San Diego on tap. The tasting area, recently remodeled and expanded, has become a very nice place to hang out.

tasting room	yes
beers on tap	15
cask / nitro	cask
tours	by request
kegs	5 & 15.5 gal.
growlers	64 & 128 oz.
bottles	12 & 22 oz.
six packs	bottles & cans
merchandise	yes
kid friendly	yes
dog friendly	no
seating	no
food	nearby

BEER	COLOR	AROMA	TASTE	
longfin lager 4.2%	light golden yellow	biscuit, bready yeasts with honey notes	light maltiness balanced by crisp light honey hops	• •
piper down 5.6% (scottish ale)	amber brown	caramel and toffee with hints of coffee	caramel, toffee balanced by a clean, crisp, slightly sweet finish	• •
chipotle black marlin porter 5.9%	dark brown	smoky chipotle and malty chocolate	smoky and spicy balanced with malty chocolate; medium mouthfeel	• •
schooner dry hopped ale 6%	medium gold	big citrus and woody hops	crisp floral, woody, and citrus hoppiness with medium body and a bitter finish	• •
dorado double IPA 10%	medium golden amber	grapefruit, citrus, honey, and floral notes	big citrus hoppiness; clean and crisp, medium bodied with a mostly bitter finish	• •

• tasters

THE BEERS AT HBM ARE CONSTANTLY rotating and changing. This is the place where wunderkind Specialty Brewer Colby Chandler has traditionally experimented with exciting variations on the Ballast Point core beers while he also brews small pilot batches of new—sometimes mind-blowing—creations that incorporate herbs, spices, fruits, and other unique ingredients. Colby now brews pilot batches at the new Ballast location (in Little Italy) but talented brewer Aaron Justus carries on the noble tradition at Home Brew Mart.

BELCHING BEAVER BREW (Vista)

belchinbeaver.com
980 Park Center Dr.
Vista, CA 92081
(760) 599-5832
Mon, Tue: Closed
Wed: 3–8 pm
Thur, Fri: 3–9 pm
Sat: 1–8 pm
Sun: 1–6 pm

1

OPENED IN 2012, BELCHING BEAVER is part of the "new wave" of breweries that have popped up in the northern third of San Diego County. Like many of their fellow brewers, Belching Beaver has taken over an industrial space within a business park and has transformed it into a 15-barrel brewery and a good-sized tasting room.

A large bar, beer-barrel tables, and a few dozen chairs service the tasting area, which shares the high-ceilinged space with fermenters and bright tanks.

tasting room	yes
beers on tap	12
cask / nitro	yes
tours	by request
kegs	5 gal.
growlers	yes
bottles	no
six packs	no
merchandise	yes
kid friendly	yes
dog friendly	yes
seating	small
food	food trucks

BEER	COLOR	AROMA	TASTE
saison de beaver 7.3%	light golden yellow	bready yeastiness	light, crisp, bready, with mild malt
blushing beaver india red ale 6%	light caramel brown	malty, caramel	hop and malt balance, caramel sweetness with crisp hops
DAM! double IPA 8.8%	reddish golden	pine and citrus	hoppy, with nice malt balance and rich mouthfeel
beavers milk stout 5.3%	dark brown	roasted coffee, chocolate, roasted malt	chocolate, malty, light bodied with rich flavors and creamy mouthfeel
honey wheat 5.5%	straw yellow	light malt character	crisp, light, with light maltiness

• tasters, half pints, pints, and flights available

FOR A RELATIVELY NEW BREWERY, Belching Beaver's brewer Troy Smith is producing an impressive array of beers and styles, and is doing them well. Locals have embraced the brewery quickly, which makes weekends at the tasting room busy, high-energy affairs that are festive, social, and not quiet.

Other locations:
North Park tasting room
4225 30th St., San Diego, CA 92104
Mon–Fri: 3 pm–9 pm
Sat and Sun: 3 pm–Midnight

BENCHMARK BREWING (Grantville)

benchmark
brewing.com
6190 Fairmount Ave.
San Diego, CA 92120
(619) 795-2111
Sun–Tue: Closed
Wed: 3 pm–8:30 pm
Thur, Fri: 3 pm–8 pm
Sat: 12 pm–8 pm

2

THIS NEW BREWERY, TUCKED INSIDE an office park, offers beer tourists another good option while cruising the Mission Valley/Friars Road area of town. Opened in June 2013, Benchmark is an inviting and casual family-run business founded by a father-and-son team of seasoned brewers and craft beer enthusiasts.

The tastefully designed space offers visitors a number of options for sitting or standing, and various charming details—such as the clever lighting fixtures at the bar, the flowers on the tables, and the satisfying and chunky tasting glasses—give Benchmark extra appeal.

tasting room	yes
beers on tap	8+
cask / nitro	cask
tours	by request
kegs	5 & 15.5 gal.
growlers	64 oz.
bottles	no
six packs	no
merchandise	yes
kid friendly	yes
dog friendly	no
seating	good
food	food trucks

BEER	COLOR	AROMA	TASTE
blonde 4.5%	light golden orange	light malty, bready with hints of honey	light, crisp, bready, with sweet honey notes, clean with a slightly sweet finish
brown ale 4.5%	amber brown	caramel, nutty, coffee notes	malty, coffee and caramel; light bodied with a mostly dry finish
oatmeal stout 4.8%	deep, dark brown	coffee, caramel, and milk chocolate	coffee and chocolate with vanilla notes; medium bodied with mostly dry finish
IPA 5.1%	medium golden	grapefruit, lemon, and honey hops	hoppy citrus with honey notes and a bitter finish
san diego 71 IPA 9.5%	medium golden	citrus and honey hops	hoppy grapefruit, lemon, and honey with a medium body and a slightly sweet finish

• tasters, half pints, pints, and flights available

BREWER MATT AKIN HAS LAUNCHED his brewery with a solid lineup of well-crafted, mostly English and American styles that offer flavor and balance—most of them at 5% ABV or lower. Surely, as the operation gets more established, a number of seasonal and specialty beers will become available.

BNS BREWING (Santee)

bnsbrewingand
distilling.com

2

10960 Wheatlands Ave.
Suite 101, Santee, CA 92071
(619) 956-0952

Sun–Thur: 12 pm–9 pm
Fri, Sat: 12 pm–10 pm

SANTEE'S THIRD OFFICIAL BREWERY, which opened its doors in June 2013, has something for almost everyone. The brewery and tasting room space also houses a homebrew supply store and the BNS distilling equipment, which offers visitors a range of spirits produced by BNS V.P. Andrew Arrabito.

The tasting area, which sports a Wild West theme, is spacious and well designed, with outdoor options (good for kids) as well as a good-sized bar and plenty of elbow-leaning options. (Check out the refrigerated copper panel that runs the length of the bar, which will keep your pint cold, if you like.)

tasting room	yes
beers on tap	4
cask / nitro	nitro
tours	no
kegs	5 & 15.5 gal.
growlers	64 oz.
bottles	no
six packs	cans
merchandise	yes
kid friendly	yes
dog friendly	no
seating	good
food	food trucks

BEER	COLOR	AROMA	TASTE
saloon girl saison 4.5%	light golden yellow	bready, yeasty esters with hints of orange peel	biscuit, honey, clove, hints of black pepper; light and crisp
gunfighter golden 5%	medium golden yellow	light malt and yeast with notes of lemon	crisp, lightly malty with honey notes and a yeasty, bready finish
flintlock pale ale 5.5%	medium golden orange	honey and citrus with hints of biscuit	full flavors of hoppy citrus, honey, and pine with medium mouthfeel and bitter finish
revolver IPA 6.5%	golden orange	citrus, pine, honey	crisp grapefruit, pine, and honey hoppiness with pleasing bitter finish

• tasters, pints, and flights available

HEAD BREWER DAN JENSEN, who learned to brew big-time at Coronado Brewing, has created an initial core lineup of 4 well-crafted and very drinkable ales, the highest ABV of which clocks in at 6.5%. With a saison, a golden, a pale ale, and an IPA, the four main styles should appeal to almost any kind of golden beer enthusiast.

BREAKWATER BREWING COMPANY (Oceanside)

breakwater
brewing.com

101 N. Coast Hwy.
Oceanside, CA 92054
(760) 433-6064

Mon–Fri: 11 am–11 pm
Sat, Sun: 11 am–12 am

1

THE OCEANSIDE VIBE IS ALL ABOUT the beach, the sun, and the surf. The folks at Breakwater Brewing have created a brewpub atmosphere that captures the laid-back feeling of the neighborhood and offers patrons a casual and friendly place to gather after a day at the beach.

A tiny brewing area is tucked away deep in the recesses of the brewpub, which is long and narrow but is sunny and offers both indoor and patio options. A long bar dominates the space, along with an impressive variety of tap handles that feature both Breakwater and guest beers.

tasting room	bar / restaurant
beers on tap	14 house / 26 guest
cask / nitro	yes
tours	no
kegs	no
growlers	64 oz.
bottles	no
six packs	no
merchandise	yes
kid friendly	yes
dog friendly	no
seating	very good
food	full menu

BEER	COLOR	AROMA	TASTE
beach honey ale 4.8%	medium golden orange	light maltiness with notes of honey and grapefruit	light maltiness, crisp and clean with a slightly bitter finish
kali kush ale 5.6%	golden yellow	sage, lavender, eucalyptus, and lemon	sage, lavender, lemon, and grapefruit; creamy mouthfeel with a mostly bitter finish
biere du jour 6% (blend of mead, honey ale, and stout)	amber brown	funky brett esters with hints of lemon	sour brett citrus followed by maltiness that finishes crisp, clean, and slightly sour
maverick's double IPA 8.4%	amber orange	big lemon and grapefruit with pine	lemon, grapefruit, pine with medium mouthfeel and bitter finish
rabiscus mead 9.6%	medium pink	raspberry and cherry	raspberry, cherry with clean, crisp slightly bubbly mouthfeel

• tasters, pints, pitchers, and flights available

BREWER LARS GILMAN LIKES TO KEEP the Breakwater lineup evolving. As an accomplished homebrewer (and owner of Hydrobrew, a homebrew shop), Lars produces a variety of styles that range from light, refreshing pale ales, to hoppy reds, to Belgian styles, stouts, and—recently—a line of sour beers. He was also one of the first brewers in San Diego to produce mead, which is also offered on site.

BUTCHER'S BREWING (Santee)

butchersbrewing.com

2

9962 Prospect Ave.
Suite E
Santee, CA 92071
(619) 334-2222
Mon: Closed
Tue–Sat: 2 pm–10 pm
Sun: 2 pm–8 pm

EXPLOSIVE GROWTH IN THE SAN DIEGO beer industry has made filling the brewery spaces in the county seem a lot like a game of musical chairs. When one brewery expands and moves out, another brewery moves in, and each brewery in the chain moves up. Such is the case with Butcher's Brewing Company, which has taken up residence in the facility that used to be home to Manzanita.

The bar and tasting room are modest in size, but nicely designed and appointed. With its low ceiling and closely spaced tables, the room can be loud, but it's a brewery, right? You don't come here to sleep.

tasting room	yes
beers on tap	15
cask / nitro	yes
tours	no
kegs	5 gal.
growlers	64 oz.
bottles	no
six packs	no
merchandise	yes
kid friendly	yes
dog friendly	no
seating	good
food	no

BEER	COLOR	AROMA	TASTE	
fairweather friend pale ale 4.45%	medium golden orange	citrus and honey hops	crisp and lightly hoppy with light mouthfeel and bitter finish	●
freerange IPA 7%	medium golden orange	honey, lemon, grapefruit	honey and citrus hop character with medium mouthfeel and nice bitter finish	●
iron hide ESB 6.5%	medium dark amber	honey and floral hops	lemon and grapefruit with medium mouthfeel and bitter finish	●●
continental breakfast stout 6.8%	dark black	chocolate, coffee, vanilla	coffee, chocolate, and vanilla with light mouthfeel and a dry finish	●●

• tasters, pints, and flights available

OWNER REY KNIGHT IS AN EXPERIENCED brewer with a good instinct for well-balanced, flavorful beers. His initial lineup includes about 10 different brews of various styles, including an ESB and a Rauchbier, as well as some specialty beers that will change on a regular basis. All in all, Butcher's offers a nicely rounded collection of beers that should have something for everyone.

CHUCKALEK INDEPENDENT BREWERS (Ramona)

chuckalek.com

2330 Main St.
Ramona, CA 92065
(513) 465-9768
Mon–Wed: Closed
Thur, Fri: 3 pm–9 pm
Sat: 12 pm–9 pm
Sun: 12 pm–8 pm

1

AS SAN DIEGO'S BEER SCENE GROWS, so does the geographical region that encompasses it. Expanding the boundaries eastward is ChuckAlek, located on the main drag (Hwy 67) in Ramona, a rural town east of Escondido.

Housed in a small strip mall–type location—along with a great butcher shop and a Thai restaurant—the ChuckAlek brewery and tasting room is a modest but comfortable place to sit and sip. Though the bar area is on the small side, a room full of tables provides plenty of options for small groups to sit down together.

tasting room	yes
beers on tap	11
cask / nitro	yes
tours	no
kegs	no
growlers	64 oz.
bottles	no
six packs	no
merchandise	yes
kid friendly	yes
dog friendly	yes
seating	good
food	food trucks & nearby

BEER	COLOR	AROMA	TASTE	
dowser altbier 5.4%	deep amber	candied sugar and toffee	caramel and raisin with a light breadiness and a slightly sweet finish	
berlinerweiss 4.5%	hazy light yellow	wheaty, bready esters with light malt	wheaty and lightly malty with a crisp, tart mouthfeel and slightly sweet finish	●
breton historic brown porter 4.7%	dark amber brown	caramel, vanilla, with coffee notes	caramel with notes of roasted malt, light bodied with a dry finish	●
la cappellana 100% brett 6%	hazy lemon yellow	funky brett esters	sour lemon and citrus with light maltiness; clean and crisp with a slightly sweet finish	●●
the hussar oak smoked wheat 5%	light yellow with a slight haze	smoky and malty with wheaty esters	smoky with hints of bacon; crisp and clean	

• tasters, pints, and flights available

OWNER/BREWER GRANT FRALEY has crafted an ambitious and fairly unique lineup of beers that you won't find at most other places. Many of his brews are reinterpretations of "old" or "historic" styles, while others combine ingredients and brewing techniques in new and interesting ways. Some beers hit the mark much more than others, but the overall effort to do things differently is worthy of praise.

CORONADO BREWING COMPANY (Coronado)

coronadobrewingcompany.com

3

170 Orange Ave.
Coronado, CA 92118
(619) 437-4452

Sun–Thur: 10:30 am–9 pm
Fri, Sat: 10:30 am–10 pm

THE ISLAND OF CORONADO (it's really a peninsula), which sits right across the bay from downtown San Diego, is a sunny, idyllic community of beach lovers, retirees, and tourists. At one end of the island sits Silver Strand beach, consistently voted one of the best beaches in the world. At the other end is Coronado Brewing Company. It is Coronado's only brewery. Luckily, it's a good one.

Both a brewpub and a brewery, Coronado has ample seating, tables, and booths for all kinds of visitors. The pub's vaguely nautical theme is enhanced by relaxed, friendly service, good food, and a nice family-centric atmosphere.

tasting room	bar / restaurant
beers on tap	15+
cask / nitro	yes
tours	yes
kegs	5 & 15.5 gal.
growlers	32 & 64 oz.
bottles	22 oz.
six packs	yes
merchandise	yes
kid friendly	yes
dog friendly	yes
seating	good
food	full menu

BEER	COLOR	AROMA	TASTE
orange ave. wit 5.2%	hazy apricot gold	honey, citrus, orange with notes of light malt	orange notes with light, malty flavors and crisp, clean, slightly sweet finish
mermaid's red 5.7%	copper amber	caramel malt with citrus hop notes	toffee malt with crisp citrus hoppiness and bitter finish with a touch of sweet
blue bridge coffee stout 5.4%	deep brown	roasted coffee	roasted coffee, light chocolate notes, light mouthfeel with a dry finish
frog's breath seasonal citrus IPA 6.5%	light golden yellow	lemongrass, lime	lemongrass with orange and citrus notes, crisp with light mouthfeel and mostly bitter finish
idiot IPA 8.5%	copper gold	citrus, pine, honey	grapefruit, lemon, honey with light mouthfeel and bitter finish

• tasters, half pints, pints, and flights available

LIKE MOST SUCCESSFUL BREWPUBS, Coronado has focused on brewing straightforward interpretations of classic beer styles, endeavoring always to make full-flavored, food-friendly brews that will appeal to a wide audience. Orange Ave. Wit, Mermaid's Red, and Idiot IPA are particularly tasty and popular selections.

CORONADO BREWING COMPANY (Bay Park)

coronadobrewing
company.com
1205 Knoxville St.
San Diego, CA 92110
(619) 275-2215
Mon–Fri: 1 pm–9 pm
Sat: 11 am–9:30 pm
Sun: 11 am–8 pm
Happy Hour Mon–Fri: 1–6

2

THIS EXPANSIVE NEW BREWERY and tasting facility, opened in spring 2013, provides a long-awaited opportunity for "mainlanders" to access Coronado beers directly from the source. Located right off Interstate 5 at Morena Boulevard, the space and equipment will also enable Coronado Brewing Company to expand production considerably—propelling them into the realm of a medium-large craft brewery.

Outfitted with a long wooden bar, long wooden "elbow" bar space, a few large tables, and plenty of seating,

tasting room	yes
beers on tap	15+
cask / nitro	yes
tours	yes
kegs	5 & 15.5 gal.
growlers	32 & 64 oz.
bottles	22 oz.
six packs	yes
merchandise	yes
kid friendly	yes
dog friendly	yes
seating	good
food	food trucks

Coronado's nicely designed tasting room is comfortable, relaxed, and friendly. There's also plenty of space for an extensive merchandise selection and a nicely stocked retail beer cooler.

IN ADDITION TO CORONADO'S SOLID core beers, an impressive variety of seasonals and specialty beers are also regularly available here. Talented brewer Shawn DeWitt offers visitors a nice range of styles to choose from, with tasty selections for hop lovers as well as malt fans and wheat-beer enthusiasts.

CULTURE BREWING CO. (Solana Beach)

culturebrewingco.com 1

111 S. Cedros Ave.
Solana Beach, CA 92075
(858) 345-1144
Mon, Tue: Closed
Wed–Fri: 3 pm–9 pm
Sat: 12 pm–9 pm
Sun: 12 pm–6 pm

OPENED IN FEBRUARY 2013, CULTURE is staking out its own unique piece of the Solana Beach brew scene. Located on the now-trendy South Cedros Avenue, just down the street from the Solana Beach train station and just up the street from the legendary Belly Up Tavern, the brewery offers shoppers, beach-goers, and music fans another quality local beer-sipping option.

The smallish tasting room is thoughtfully designed—elegant and contemporary, with a few tables and stools. (The tasting glasses are particularly cool.) The outdoor space in back, open to the brewhouse and fermentation

tasting room	yes
beers on tap	12+
cask / nitro	cask
tours	no
kegs	yes
growlers	yes
bottles	no
six packs	no
merchandise	yes
kid friendly	no
dog friendly	yes
seating	tables
food	nearby

BEER	COLOR	AROMA	TASTE
amber ale 5.2%	orange-amber	caramel malt	malt forward, nice hops, medium-light mouthfeel
pale ale 5.8%	golden yellow	honey and malt, light hops	malt forward with crisp, refreshing hop finish
American brown 6.0%	dark caramel brown	malty, roasty, floral hops	rich, malty backbone balanced by nice crisp hoppiness on the finish
black IPA 7.2%	dark caramel brown	citrus and floral hops	rich, deep flavor balanced by citrus and floral hoppiness
imperial stout 9.2%	deep, dark brown	roasty, chocolate, hints of vanilla	malty roastiness, chocolate, hints of coffee, dry up front with slightly sweet finish

• tasters, pints, and flights available

tanks, offers a good-sized area for standing, sipping, and shooting the breeze.

CLASSIC AMERICAN BEER STYLES, brewed by Steve Ragan and Dennis Williams, make up the core of the Culture lineup, with a through-line of nicely balanced beers that finish with pleasing crispness and hop balance. With beers that are easy to drink and refreshing on the palate, this fledgling brewery has a bright future.

ARCANA BREWING (FORMERLY FEZZIWIG'S) (Carlsbad)

arcanabrewing.com
5621 Palmer Way
Carlsbad, CA 92010
(909) 529-2337
Mon–Wed: Closed
Thur: 4 pm–6 pm
Fri: 3:30 pm–9 pm
Sat: 1:30 pm–7 pm
Sun: 1:30 pm–6 pm

FIRST OPENED LATE IN 2012, Arcana is one of many small-batch breweries that have sprung from the dreams of a motivated young San Diego homebrewer.

The long, narrow tasting room has ample space, with a long bar and plenty of places to stand and rest your pint. The tasting room is open to the brewing area, which displays the small tanks, malt bags, and brewing system that produce the brewery's product.

tasting room	yes
beers on tap	10
cask / nitro	nitro
tours	no
kegs	no
growlers	yes
bottles	no
six packs	no
merchandise	yes
kid friendly	no
dog friendly	yes
seating	fair
food	weekend food trucks

BEER	COLOR	AROMA	TASTE
tiny tim cream ale 4.8%	light golden straw	light malt, floral	light maltiness, crisp
ebenezer IPA 6.4%	reddish caramel	floral hops, malt	malt forward, mellow, low bitterness
bitter nut brown 4.6%	reddish caramel brown	caramel, sweet malt	light maltiness
annabelles umber 5.2%	brownish red	malty, caramel	light, roasty malt with hints of chocolate
darby porter 4.8%	dark brown	cocoa, chocolate	light, roasty malt with hints of chocolate
dark xmas 8.1%	deep brown	roasted malt, chocolate	toffee and chocolate notes, light mouthfeel

• tasters, pints, and flights available

LIKE MANY A SMALL UPSTART VENTURE, Arcana will do a rotating selection of small-batch beers that satisfy the passions and tastes of the brewer. Founder and Brewmaster Daniel Guy currently plans to produce about 250 barrels per year on his 3.5-barrel system, and he will concentrate mostly on brewing his versions of traditional English-style ales.

GORDON BIERSCH BREWERY RESTAURANT (Mission Valley)

gordonbiersch.com

2

5010 Mission Center Rd.
San Diego, CA 92108

(619) 688-1120

Sun–Thur: 11 am–1 am
Fri, Sat: 11 am–2 am

SAN DIEGO'S GORDON BIERSCH is a testament to the fact that a large brewery-restaurant can be owned by a big corporation, yet still maintain a high level of beer quality. A good deal of credit for that goes to master brewer Doug Hasker, who's been lending his considerable talent to Gordon Biersch for more than 20 years.

Gordon Biersch's space is quite large, and offers a variety of seating options for patrons. A huge indoor dining area opens out onto an inviting outdoor patio space, and special private rooms are also available for large parties.

tasting room	bar / restaurant
beers on tap	7
cask / nitro	no
tours	by request
kegs	5 & 15.5 gal.
growlers	64 oz. & 2 liter
bottles	no
six packs	no
merchandise	yes
kid friendly	yes
dog friendly	no
seating	large
food	full menu

BEER	COLOR	AROMA	TASTE
golden export lager 5%	light golden yellow	light European malts with hop notes	light malt with notes of honey; crisp and clean with a mostly bitter finish
hefeweizen 5.5%	hazy golden banana yellow	clove, banana, notes of black pepper	banana, clove, pepper; creamy mouthfeel with crisp, slightly sweet finish
Czech pilsner 5.6%	medium golden	honey, bready malt, notes of spice	honey, malt, crisp and clean with notes of spice
marzen 5.7%	amber copper	caramel, toffee with notes of floral hops	caramel, toffee with crisp hoppy notes and a medium-sweet finish
schwarzbier 4.3%	medium chocolate brown	bready, caramel, roasted coffee and chocolate notes	coffee, caramel, with light mouthfeel, mostly bitter finish with slight trailing sweetness
blonde bock 7%	light golden honey	light European malts with honey hop notes	light, crisp with malty and floral hop flavors, bitter finish

• tasters, pints, and flights available

DOUG HASKER'S BEER LINEUP is distinctly Bavarian-centric, and he is well established as one of San Diego's premiere lager brewers. All his beers are crafted according to the strict standards of the *Reinheitsgebot* (German Purity Law of 1516), and most utilize traditional European hops and malts. Fans of crisp, clean, malt-forward brews should not miss an opportunity to taste this expert portfolio.

GREEN FLASH BREWING CO. (Mira Mesa)

greenflashbrew.com
6550 Mira Mesa Blvd.
San Diego, CA 92121
(858) 622-0085
Mon: Closed
Tue–Thur: 3 pm–9 pm
Fri: 3 pm–10 pm
Sat: 12 pm–9 pm
Sun: 12 pm–6 pm

2

GREEN FLASH IS ONE OF SAN DIEGO'S happy success stories. Within a span of less than 9 years, they went from being a small 13,000-barrel brewery in Vista to a 75,000-barrel (232,500-gallon) powerhouse in Mira Mesa.

Walking into Green Flash feels like walking into a majestic old European cathedral—not from a style standpoint, but from a space standpoint. Inside its more than 45,000 square feet, pallets of beer are stacked like columns, rising toward the 30-foot ceiling. Huge slabs of concrete enclose various areas that clink with the sound of glass bottles and thud with the sound of cardboard cases in motion. And right in the middle

tasting room	yes
beers on tap	20
cask / nitro	cask
tours	wed–sun
kegs	5 & 15.5 gal.
growlers	32 & 64 oz.
bottles	22 oz.
six packs	4 packs
merchandise	yes
kid friendly	yes
dog friendly	yes
seating	outside
food	food trucks every day

BEER	COLOR	AROMA	TASTE
west coast IPA 7.3%	deep golden copper	grapefruit, citrus hops	citrus hoppiness balanced by caramel malts, lingering bitterness and finishes dry
hop head red 7%	medium dark reddish copper	caramel malt, citrus hops	sweet caramel, toffee balanced by crisp citrus, touch of sweet but finishes dry
double stout 8.8%	deep dark brown	roasted chocolate, vanilla	rich, roasty malty sweetness, chocolate, with a creamy mouthfeel, finishes semi-dry
le freak 9.2% (Belgian-style ale)	light copper, straw yellow	banana, fruity esters, lemon and guava	malty up front, with bready Belgian yeastiness and a crisp citrus, hoppy finish
trippel 9.7%	golden yellow	fruity esters, tropical fruit, banana, bubble gum, bready yeast	light, crisp mouthfeel that delivers tropical fruit, grapefruit, banana, balanced by crisp hoppiness

• tasters, half pints, and pints available

of all this activity is a cavernous tasting room with extensive bar space (no seats), a friendly team of certified beer servers, and a large selection of great beers.

THANKS TO THE WORK OF MASTER BREWER Chuck Silva, Green Flash is one of those breweries that covers all styles, pleases all palates, and does everything well. Though they are beloved by hop-heads for their various bold IPAs, they also have a huge following among fans of Belgian-style beers, barleywines, and stouts.

HELM'S BREWING (Kearny Mesa)

helmsbrewingco.com
5640 Kearny Mesa Rd.
San Diego, CA 92111
(858) 384-2772
Mon, Tue: Closed
Wed, Thur: 3 pm–8 pm
Fri: 3 pm–9 pm
Sat: 12 pm–9 pm
Sun: 12 pm–7 pm

2

FIRST OPENED IN THE FALL OF 2012, this microbrewery joined the quickly growing brewery population of the Clairemont/Kearny Mesa area, just off the 163 freeway. Tucked into a business park setting, as so many are, Helm's has a relatively large space for tasting.

In among the brewhouse, tanks, and barrels is a long bar and an additional long beer ledge that provides ample standing and sitting space space for guests.

tasting room	yes
beers on tap	9
cask / nitro	nitro
tours	no
kegs	5 & 15.5 gal.
growlers	yes
bottles	no
six packs	no
merchandise	yes
kid friendly	no
dog friendly	yes
seating	fair
food	weekend food trucks

BEER	COLOR	AROMA	TASTE
captain's pale 6.0%	golden yellow	floral hops	light malt, hops, light mouthfeel
wicked as sin IPA 6.6%	golden yellow	notes of pine, citrus	malt/hop balance, medium mouthfeel
hop the RIPA 7.2%	dark amber	toffee, caramel, honey	notes of butterscotch, caramel, malt, finishes bitter
beerachino 7.3%	dark brown	coffee, malt, and chocolate	roasty malt, hints of chocolate, notes of pepper on the finish
en garde 6.9%	deep orange	bready, tropical Belgian yeast	orange, spice, hints of clove

- tasters, pints, and flights available

THE INITIAL LINEUP AT HELM'S is a mishmash of styles that focuses on working to make accessible, easy-to-drink brews that will appeal to a wide range of people. Regulars on tap include a pale ale, a few variations of IPA, a Belgian-inspired option or two, and a couple of dark, porter-like selections.

MIKE HESS BREWING (Miramar/North Park)

hessbrewing.com

3

3812 Grim Ave.
San Diego, CA 92104
(619) 786-HESS
Sun–Tue: Closed
Wed, Thur: 2 pm–7 pm
Fri: 2 pm–8 pm
Sat: 1 pm–7 pm

WHEN MIKE HESS FIRST ROLLED UP the garage doors at his tiny 20' x 30' office park space and began pouring for the public, the longtime homebrewer was still making beer in 1.6-barrel (51-gallon) batches. Though he wanted to take it slow, the beer-drinking public made it nearly impossible for the brewery to stay small.

To answer the demand from his fans, Hess opened a gorgeous new 13,000-square-foot facility in North Park in August 2013. The impressive and smartly designed two-story brewery and tasting facility houses a 30-barrel system and 8 fermenters.

tasting room	yes
beers on tap	10+
cask / nitro	yes
tours	by request
kegs	5 gal. & 50 liter
growlers	1 & 2 liter
bottles	no
six packs	4 packs cans
merchandise	yes
kid friendly	yes
dog friendly	yes
seating	very good
food	food trucks & nearby

BEER	COLOR	AROMA	TASTE
claritas 5.8% (kolsch)	medium golden yellow	light malt with hints of honey and warm bread	light maltiness with notes of honey; clean and crisp with a bitter finish
pallidus 6.3% (Belgian pale ale)	medium golden orange	bready Belgian esters, spice, and clove	breadty esters, spice, clove, with hints of orange; crisp, mostly bitter finish
grazias 6.3% (Vienna cream ale)	deep amber	big caramel, toffee malt	roasted coffee, caramel, toffee; nicely balanced with a mostly sweet finish
habitus 8% (rye IPA)	medium golden orange	honey and pine	honey with pine notes, medium mouthfeel with a mostly bitter finish
ex umbris 10.2% (stout)	deep dark brown	chocolate, caramel, toffee with hints of vanilla	milk chocolate, roasted coffee, caramel, with vanilla notes; rich mouthfeel with balanced sweet and bitter finish

- tasters, pints, and flights available

MIKE AND HIS HEAD BREWER, Nate Sampson, have developed a tasty lineup that includes a nice selection of malty and hoppy creations, along with a few beers (like their Vienna cream ale) that are unique to San Diego.

Other locations:
7955 Silverton Ave. #1201, San Diego, CA 92126
(619) 786-4377
Sun–Tue: Closed; Wed, Thur: 2 pm–7 pm
Fri: 2 pm–8 pm; Sat: 1 pm–7 pm

HILLCREST BREWING COMPANY (Hillcrest)

hillcrestbrewing
company.com

3

1458 University Ave.
San Diego, CA 92103
(619) 269-4323

Mon–Fri: 4 pm–12 am
Sat, Sun: 12 pm–12 am

TUCKED INTO THE CORNER OF A SMALLISH strip mall in the heart of Hillcrest, this brewery—which bills itself as the "world's first openly gay brewery"—offers a big, open, and well-designed space that is inviting to families, dogs, bikes, and all kinds of beer fans. One of the newcomers from the class of 2012, Hillcrest Brewing appears to have been embraced by the locals in this generally hip, trendy, and artsy neighborhood.

Inside, a big curvy bar offers plenty of seating, along with a number of large, sturdy family-style tables. A nice-sized outdoor patio provides still another sit-down option for drinking or dining on tasty pizzas, wings, and salads.

tasting room	bar / restaurant
beers on tap	24
cask / nitro	no
tours	no
kegs	5 & 15.5 gal.
growlers	64 oz. & 1 gal.
bottles	no
six packs	no
merchandise	yes
kid friendly	yes
dog friendly	outdoors
seating	plentiful
food	pizza, wings & salads

BEER	COLOR	AROMA	TASTE
hefeweizen 5%	hazy golden yellow	big banana, clove, bready yeast	crisp, with big banana, clove, and spice
lucy brown ale 4.5%	dark brown	sweet maltiness with hints of chocolate	rich malt with hints of sweet chocolate, finishes dry with a light mouthfeel
Russian imperial stout 11%	deep, dark brown	light hints of roasted coffee and chocolate	light mouthfeel with hints of chocolate and roasted malts
hoppy endings IPA 7.5%	medium, reddish caramel	floral hops, with hints of sweet caramel malt	good hoppiness, medium body, light mouthfeel

- tasters, pints, and flights available

BREWER AND FOUNDER

David White offers a straightforward lineup of food-friendly, accessible beers, which include familiar and popular styles, such as Hefeweizen, a brown ale, an IPA, a Scotch Ale, and Russian Imperial Stout.

INDIAN JOE BEER (Vista)

indianjoebeer.com
2379 La Mirada Dr.
Vista, CA 92081
(760) 295-3945
Mon, Tue: Closed
Wed: 4 pm–7 pm
Thur, Fri: 3 pm–9 pm
Sat: 12 pm–9 pm
Sun: 12 pm–6 pm

1

INDIAN JOE JOINED THE SYCAMORE WAY brewing community in Vista at the end of 2012. Started by veteran homebrewer Max Moran, this brewery is the fulfillment of a longtime dream. Moran claims to be the first (and only) Native American pro brewer in the country (he is Luiseño Indian).

Tucked into a light industrial office park, Indian Joe's tasting room has a quaint, informal, homey feeling. There are good seating options with stools, a smallish bar, and a number of tables for 6 or more. Old black-and-white historical photos of Moran's family adorn the walls, as do other Native American graphics.

tasting room	yes
beers on tap	28
cask / nitro	nitro
tours	by request
kegs	no
growlers	64 oz.
bottles	no
six packs	no
merchandise	yes
kid friendly	yes
dog friendly	yes
seating	good
food	wed–sun food trucks

BEER	COLOR	AROMA	TASTE
American Indian IPA 5.7%	light golden orange	citrus, orange, grapefruit	crisp citrus flavors with notes of spice and sage; finishes medium bitter
American Indian red ale 5.8%	medium dark copper orange	caramel malt and toffee	caramel and toffee with a crisp light mouthfeel; finishes semi-sweet
American Indian IPA 8.3%	deep orange	big citrus and floral hops	grapefruit, orange, notes of pine and grass; crisp, finishes bitter
463 American Indian pale ale 8.7%	golden orange	citrus hops with floral notes	orange, grapefruit, lemon, with crisp hoppiness, light mouthfeel, and bitter finish
black IPA 6.5%	deep, inky brown	roasted malt and coffee	roasted chocolate and coffee, medium mouthfeel; clean bitter finish

- tasters, pints, and flights available

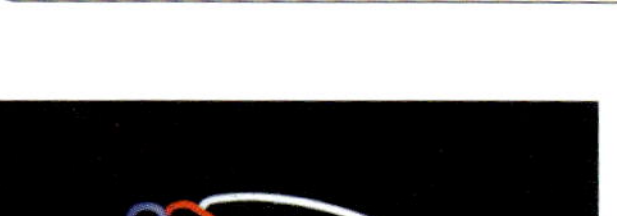

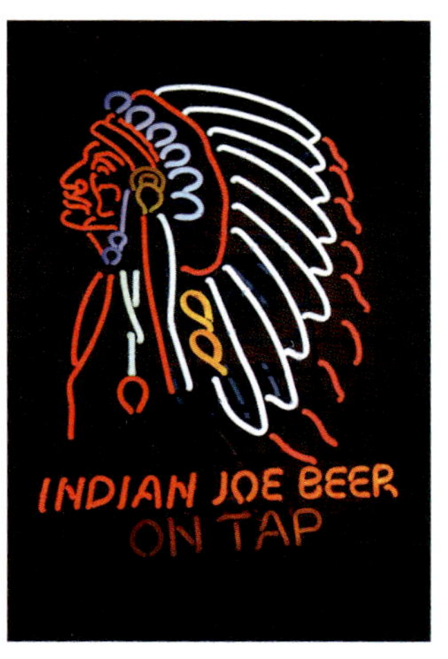

MORAN BREWS AN AMBITIOUS lineup of beers, and he does it on a very small system. He's got more than two dozen of his own brews on tap at all times, and—like many a homebrewer—he likes to move around from style to style quite freely. In addition to his more straightforward brews, he offers a number of options with more unusual flavors, such as wheat beers flavored with apricot, peach, red raspberry, orange, and honey.

INTERGALACTIC BREWING COMPANY (Miramar)

intergalacticbrew.com ❷
9835 Carroll Centre Rd.
Suite #108
San Diego, CA 92126
(858) 750-0601
Sun–Tue: Closed
Wed, Thur: 3 pm–8 pm
Fri: 3 pm–9 pm
Sat: 12 pm–6 pm

SOMETIMES, GOOD THINGS DO COME IN small packages. This nano rolled up its garage door in April 2013 and started offering its brews to the public—one 20-gallon batch at a time. Though the tasting room and brewery are a bit of a challenge to find (tucked away in the back of an industrial office park), the search will reap tasty rewards.

The modest tasting room is outfitted with a small bar and a few spaces to lean against—but mostly it's about standing and sipping.

tasting room	yes
beers on tap	8
cask / nitro	nitro
tours	no
kegs	no
growlers	32 & 64 oz.
bottles	no
six packs	no
merchandise	yes
kid friendly	yes
dog friendly	yes
seating	limited
food	nearby

BEER	COLOR	AROMA	TASTE
subspace session ale 4%	light yellow	floral and citrus hops	light, crisp
andromeda IPA 6.8%	medium golden orange	honey and citrus roasted malts	honey and citrus balanced by crisp hoppy bitterness; medium mouthfeel
orion's stout 5.8%	deep dark brown	chocolate, coffee	milk chocolate and coffee maltiness; light mouthfeel with dry finish
reentry smoked ale 5.1% (rauch smoked pale ale)	medium gold	peppers, green pepper, smoky peat	smoky with good serrano flavor; crisp with balanced spicy finish
space oasis coconut porter 6.9%	deep dark brown	roasted coffee, chocolate, and coconut	coconut and chocolate flavors balanced by light mouthfeel and dry finish
black sun 8.5% (black IPA)	deep dark black	citrus and pine	big hoppy citrus and floral character balanced by dark malt and mostly bitter finish

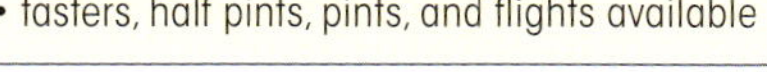

• tasters, half pints, pints, and flights available

BEFORE OPENING INTERGALACTIC, owner/brewer Alex Van Horne was already well respected in the homebrewing community. He's ventured out to the public with an ambitious array of 8 core beers, some of which display an impressive ability to use flavorings in a restrained and thoughtful way (the Serrano Rauch beer and the Coconut Porter being two good examples). Kudos to a tiny brewery of this size that can produce beers of this quality.

IRON FIST BREWING COMPANY (Vista)

ironfistbrewing.com
1305 Hot Spring Way
#101, Vista, CA 92081
(760) 216-6500
Mon, Tue: 4 pm–8 pm
Wed: Closed
Thur, Fri: 3 pm–8 pm
Sat: 12 pm–6 pm
Sun: 12 pm–5 pm

WHEN IRON FIST FIRST OPENED in 2010, they hit the ground running with a 15-barrel brewhouse and an aggressive plan for growth. Fortunately, they've never looked back. Embraced by legions of craft beer fans, Iron Fist has been expanding space, adding tanks, and ramping up production at a dizzying pace.

The recently expanded brewery and tasting room, opened in July 2012, offers visitors a roomy but mostly standing-room venue set among the rows of fermentation tanks and tall racks of barrels. Friendly service and a fun, casual vibe are the product of a family-centered business built by a brewer son, his parents, and his grandparents.

tasting room	yes
beers on tap	12
cask / nitro	nitro
tours	by request
kegs	5 & 15.5 gal.
growlers	64 oz.
bottles	375 & 750 ml.
six packs	no
merchandise	yes
kid friendly	yes
dog friendly	yes
seating	good
food	wed–sun food trucks

BEER	COLOR	AROMA	TASTE
renegade blonde 5.2% (kolsch style)	light golden yellow	light German malts and breadiness with notes of citrus	light bready malt balanced with crisp hoppy notes; balanced and finishes with light bitterness
hired hand 6.5% (saison style)	golden yellow	coriander, citrus and bready esters	orange peel, spice, warm malt balanced with a crisp light mouthfeel
dubbel fisted 8% (Belgian style dubbel)	medium copper red	Belgian yeasty esters, spice, caramel	tropical fruit, dry fruit, buble gum, with a malty semi-sweet finish
gauntlet double IPA 9.5%	medium golden orange	bright citrus, grapefruit, orange hop notes	rich orange, grapefruit, pine with medium mouthfeel and crisp bitter finish
velvet glove 9% (imperial oatmeal stout)	deep, dark brown	roasted malt, chocolate, and coffee	roasted coffee, chocolate, with hints of vanilla and liqueur; finishes semi-sweet

• tasters, pints, and flights available

BREWMASTER BRANDON SIEMINSKI has the distinction of being one of San Diego's youngest pro brewers (Iron Fist opened when he turned 21), but his level of talent and creativity go far beyond his years. Excellent Belgian-inspired ales are probably the backbone of the Iron Fist lineup, but the brewery also produces a delicious saison, imperial IPA, and stout, as well as excellent specialty beers.

JULIAN BREWING COMPANY (Julian)

baileybbq.com

2307 Main St.
Julian, CA 92036
(760) 765-3757

Sun–Thur: 11:30 am–9 pm
Fri: 11:30 am–11 pm
Sat: 11:30 am–midnight

1

BACK IN THE 1800s, WHEN JULIAN was primarily a mining town, Julian Brewing Company became its first brewery. It had been closed down for quite a while before Vince Marsaglia (key member of the Pizza Port dynasty) and his business partners decided to revive the name and the business, along with reviving the Bailey BBQ restaurant, which adjoins the small brewery.

The brewery's tasting room is part of the BBQ restaurant; and the casual, friendly, family-oriented dining areas are all about high-quality fare in a no-frills package. Indoor and outdoor seating options are plentiful, as are delicious pit-smoked meats and homemade sides of all kinds.

tasting room	bar / restaurant
beers on tap	7 house / 9 guest
cask / nitro	nitro
tours	by request
kegs	no
growlers	no
bottles	no
six packs	no
merchandise	yes
kid friendly	yes
dog friendly	yes
seating	very good
food	full menu

BEER	COLOR	AROMA	TASTE
cedar creek honey ale 5.4%	golden honey	light malts, honey, with hints of nuts	light, sweet maltiness, with honey notes and slightly sweet finish; crisp and clean
dark farmhouse saison 5.5%	deep amber brown	bready esters, spice, and orange peel	spices, clove, bready with malty, mostly bitter finish
amber 6.6%	deep amber	caramel, toffee	caramel and toffee with a light mouthfeel and slightly sweet finish
IPA 7.5%	golden yellow	big pineapple, citrus, and pine	lemon, pineapple, and citrus with hints of pine and a bitter finish

• tasters, pints, pitchers, and flights available

BREWER MIKE GABBARD offers visitors a good selection of solid, well-crafted beers that are brewed on the premises, focused mostly on traditional American and English styles. Though all the beers pair exceedingly well with the food, the IPAs are particularly flavorful and satisfying.

Restaurant Hours:
11:30 am–8:30 pm

KARL STRAUSS (MAIN PRODUCTION BREWERY) (Pacific Beac

karlstrauss.com
5985 Santa Fe St.
San Diego, CA 92109
(858) 273-2739
Mon, Tue: Closed
Wed: 2 pm–8 pm
Thur, Fri: 2 pm–9 pm
Sat: 12 pm–9 pm
Sun: 12 pm–5 pm

IN AUGUST 2013, KARL STRAUSS'S production brewery finally realized its longtime dream of opening a tasting room on site. And it was worth waiting for. The large, airy, nicely designed space houses a long bar, a barrel room area, and generous seating along with a beautiful outdoor patio/beer garden.

Inside, visitors can peek through various windows to watch the bottling line in action, or to glimpse some of the other workings in the brewing area. Television monitors also provide a sort of "Karl TV" streaming into the tasting space, which is a fun way to make the mostly off-limits brewery accessible to visitors.

tasting room	yes
beers on tap	20
cask / nitro	cask
tours	by request
kegs	5 & 15.5 gal.
growlers	64 oz. & 1 liter
bottles	12 & 22 oz.
six packs	yes
merchandise	yes
kid friendly	yes
dog friendly	no
seating	very good
food	food trucks

BEER	COLOR	AROMA	TASTE
karl strauss amber 4.2%	deep golden orange	light bready malt with notes of citrus and floral hops	light bready caramel malt balanced by light hops; slightly sweet finish
red trolley ale 5.8%	reddish copper	caramel, toffee, hints of dry fruit	caramel, toffee, hints of vanilla, medium bodied, crisp with a slightly sweet finish
tower 10 IPA 7%	deep golden yellow	hoppy pine and citrus with hints of grapefruit	citrus and grapefruit, crisp and clean with a mostly bitter finish
big barrel double IPA 9%	dark golden orange	bright citrus, grapefruit, orange hop notes balanced with caramel malt	orange, grapefruit, pine hoppiness with medium mouthfeel and crisp bitter finish

• tasters, pints, and flights available

PATRONS WILL ENJOY A DRAFT selection of about 20 beers, including some of the specialty and seasonal batches that get only limited release outside of the Karl Strauss company.

KARL STRAUSS DOWNTOWN (Downtown)

karlstrauss.com

3

1157 Columbia St.
San Diego, CA 92101
(619) 234-2739
Mon–Thur: 11 am–11 pm
Fri: 11 am–midnight
Sat: 11:30 am–midnight
Sun: 11:30 am–10 pm

THE MODERN ERA OF SAN DIEGO'S craft beer history began with Karl Strauss. When founders Chris Cramer and Matt Rattner opened their doors in 1989, they were the only craft brewery in San Diego. They were also faced with the onerous task of convincing the world that craft beer is better than mass-produced beer. Thanks in large part to their hard work, the craft beer scene is thriving.

The Karl Strauss lineup is an impressive portfolio that spans classic American, English, and Belgian styles. All in all, the brewery brews more than 30 different beers a year. Highly talented Brewmaster Paul Segura has done

tasting room	bar / restaurant
beers on tap	10+
cask / nitro	cask
growlers	64 oz.
bottles	22 oz.
six packs	no
merchandise	yes
kid friendly	yes
dog friendly	outside patio
seating	very good
food	full menu

an excellent job of maintaining the “classic” recipes while also producing an impressive variety of specialty beers that blend unique ingredients and techniques. If you happen to spot any of his anniversary or holiday beers in bottles, you’d do well to snatch them up.

KARL STRAUSS 4S RANCH (4S Ranch)

karlstrauss.com

1

10448 Reserve Dr.
San Diego, CA 92127

(858) 376-2739

Sun–Thur: 11 am–10 pm
Fri, Sat: 11 am–11 pm

tasting room	bar / restaurant
beers on tap	10+
cask / nitro	cask
growlers	64 oz.
bottles	22 oz.
six packs	no
merchandise	yes
kid friendly	yes
dog friendly	outside patio
seating	very good
food	full menu

ONE OF THE newest Karl Strauss brewpubs to open, this location is a testament to the idea that if you do it right, people will come. The site, which first housed a "pub-flavored" chain restaurant that went out of business, is now booming. A large bar, spacious interior, and welcoming outdoor patio (complete with fire pit) make for a comfortable and friendly atmosphere that suits friends and family alike.

KARL STRAUSS CARLSBAD (Carlsbad)

karlstrauss.com

5801 Armada Dr.
Carlsbad, CA 92008

(760) 431-2739

Sun–Thur: 7 am–10 pm
Fri, Sat: 7 am–11 pm

1

tasting room	bar / restaurant
beers on tap	10+
cask / nitro	cask
growlers	64 oz.
bottles	22 oz.
six packs	no
merchandise	yes
kid friendly	yes
dog friendly	no
seating	very good
food	full menu

KARL'S CARLSBAD location sits atop a hill in an office park environment, where the spacious restaurant is often filled with professionals for lunch. A small brewing system enhances the overall ambiance, which is light, modern, and family-friendly.

KARL STRAUSS LA JOLLA (La Jolla)

karlstrauss.com

2

1044 Wall St.
La Jolla, CA 92037
(858) 551-2739

Mon–Wed: 11 am–9 pm
Thur–Sat: 11 am–10 pm
Sun: 11 am–9 pm

tasting room	bar / restaurant
beers on tap	10+
cask / nitro	cask
growlers	64 oz.
bottles	22 oz.
six packs	no
merchandise	yes
kid friendly	yes
dog friendly	outside patio
seating	very good
food	full menu

OPEN AND AIRY, with a classy contemporary design, this Karl Strauss location sits in the heart of downtown La Jolla proper. A variety of seating options abound, from booths to large tables, to bar seating, to outdoor patio tables. A large bar offers 10 to 12 Karl Strauss brews on tap, almost always including a seasonal and sometimes a specialty beer, and the full menu is always available.

KARL STRAUSS SORRENTO MESA (Sorrento Mesa)

karlstrauss.com
9675 Scranton Rd.
San Diego, CA 92121
(858) 587-2739

2

Mon–Wed: 11 am–9 pm
Thur, Fri: 11 am–10 pm
Sat: Closed
Sun: 10 am–2 pm

tasting room	bar / restaurant
beers on tap	10+
cask / nitro	cask
growlers	64 oz.
bottles	22 oz.
six packs	no
merchandise	yes
kid friendly	yes
dog friendly	outside patio
seating	very good
food	full menu

NESTLED INTO a corporate office park not far off Mira Mesa Boulevard, this large family-friendly location is the Karl Strauss hidden gem. If you didn't know to look for it, you could very well never know it was there. Set back on a path, and camouflaged by foliage, the restaurant offers a number of charming features, including outdoor patio areas that overlook a beautiful koi pond.

LATITUDE 33 BREWING COMPANY (Vista)

1

lat33brew.com
1430 Vantage Ct.
#104, Vista, CA 92081
(760) 913-7333
(855) 598-2337 (Toll Free)
Mon–Wed: Closed
Thur, Fri: 3pm–8pm
Sat: 12pm–6pm
Sun: 12pm–5pm

THE FOLKS AT LATITUDE 33 inherited a major legacy when they moved into what used to be the old Green Flash brewery. Needless to say, a lot of great beer has been brewed here and, well, Latitude 33 feels the pressure—but in a good way.

They're still growing into the space (albeit very quickly), but Latitude 33 has created a nice, large tasting area—in among the tanks—where visitors can stand and enjoy pints and tasters. The room is relatively bare bones, but there's plenty of room to move around.

tasting room	yes
beers on tap	9
cask / nitro	no
tours	by request
kegs	5 & 15.5 gal.
growlers	64 oz.
bottles	22 oz.
six packs	no
merchandise	yes
kid friendly	yes
dog friendly	yes
seating	no
food	food trucks

BEER	COLOR	AROMA	TASTE
g.b. pale ale 5%	medium orange	citrus and pine	light citrus and pine with a clean, crisp maltiness and a bitter finish
strawhorse wheat ale 5.2%	golden yellow	light malts and honey	lightly malty with honey notes; crisp with a slightly sweet finish
pasha's rye brown 6%	medium brown	caramel and roasted malt	caramel, toffee, and roasted coffee with chocolate notes; crisp with a dry finish
vanilla's porter 6.5%	deep reddish brown	roasted coffee and vanilla	coffee, roasted malt, and vanilla; medium bodied with a slightly sweet finish
camel corps IPA 6.8%	medium orange	pine and citrus	lemon and grapefruit; light and crisp with a bitter finish

- tasters, half pints, pints, and flights available

BREWER AND FOUNDER KEVIN BUCKLEY offers a nice range of beers that, as he says, takes traditional styles and gives them a Southern California twist. His German-style pils, for example, uses West Coast hops (he also does a very tasty version that's dry-hopped).

LIGHTNING BREWERY (Poway)

lightningbrewery.com

1

13200 Kirkham Way
Poway, CA 92064

(858) 513-8070

Fri: 1:30 pm–7 pm
Sat, Sun: 1 pm–5 pm

ALTHOUGH "BETTER BEER THROUGH SCIENCE" is the official motto for Lightning Brewery, it belies the fact that there's also a lot of true passion at the brewery's core. To the naked eye, Lightning still seems small, but its production is booming and its popularity is growing fast.

Located in a small office park in Poway, Lightning is a bit off the beaten brewery tour path, but it's well worth the trip. A large, new cold box and a brand-new tasting room dominate the area next to the brewery, where visitors can stand, sip, and taste in an intimate but ample space.

tasting room	yes
beers on tap	8+
cask / nitro	no
tours	by request
kegs	5 & 15.5 gal.
growlers	64 oz.
bottles	22 oz.
six packs	yes
merchandise	yes
kid friendly	no
dog friendly	no
seating	no
food	weekend food trucks

BEER	COLOR	AROMA	TASTE
thunderweizen 5.5% (hefeweizen)	deep hazy golden yellow	banana, clove, citrus, allspice, biscuit	banana, clove, tropical fruit; crisp with silky mouthfeel
elemental pilsner 5.6%	medium golden yellow	light malts and fresh hops	clean, crisp hops balanced by light maltiness and hints of spice
ionizer lager 8.3%	deep golden yellow	light floral hops and malts	medium body, malt forward balanced by crisp hops and semi-dry finish
electrostatic ale 10% (farmhouse ale)	deep copper	spicy hops, light malts, bready yeast and fruity esters	fruit and biscuit with good malt backbone and sourness
old tempestuous ale 9%	dark reddish golden	roasted malts, fruity esters, sherry, dried fruit, light hops	spicy, rich toffee and caramel, raisins, crisp hops; rich mouthfeel
black lightning porter 8.5%	dark, inky brown	roasted coffee and caramel	toffee, caramel, bitter chocolate and roasted coffee notes balanced by smooth bitterness

• tasters available

OWNER AND FOUNDER Jim Crute, a biochemist by trade, wants Lightning to provide a haven for beer lovers who don't necessarily crave bitter brews that so many others in San Diego brew, and do very well. With his traditional focus on lagers, Jim has crafted an impressive lineup of more malt-forward beers that are sure to please drinkers who have yet to embrace the super-hopped, high-IBU IPAs and double IPAs. Hef fans should not miss the chance to taste the full-flavored, banana-clove–laden Thunderweizen, which is considered by many to be one of the best hefs in San Diego.

MANZANITA BREWING COMPANY (Santee)

manzanitabrewing.com
10151 Prospect Ave.
Santee, CA 92071
(619) 334-1757
Mon, Tue: Closed
Wed, Thur: 4 pm–8 pm
Fri: 4 pm–10 pm
Sat: 1 pm–10 pm
Sun: 1 pm–6 pm

2

IN 2010, WHEN MANZANITA BECAME Santee's first brewery, they gave the locals near the eastern edge of San Diego something to cheer about. After only a few years in their original space—producing 1,200 barrels a year in 3,000 square feet—the brewery was forced to find larger accommodations so it could expand to meet the quickly growing demand.

The new production brewery and current tasting room (now more than 12,000 square feet), which opened in July 2012, is a nicely designed, welcoming space dominated by a long wooden bar and plenty of stools. Bar tables and chairs provide additional places to pull up and enjoy a beer.

tasting room	yes
beers on tap	12
cask / nitro	cask
tours	by request
kegs	5 & 15.5 gal.
growlers	2 liter
bottles	22 oz.
six packs	no
merchandise	yes
kid friendly	yes
dog friendly	outside patio
seating	good
food	weekend food trucks

BEER	COLOR	AROMA	TASTE
riverwalk blonde 6%	medium golden orange	light bready yeast and German malt	crisp, light breadiness and maltiness with a clean, mildly bitter finish
rustic horizon red 6.8%	dark amber red	caramel and toffee maltiness	caramel malt, light mouthfeel with a crisp, mostly bitter finish
gillespie brown 9.5%	dark brown with orange tones	toffee and caramel, with a hint of coffee	caramel malt, chocolate with a medium mouthfeel and bitter finish
chaotic double IPA 10.1%	medium golden orange	citrus, honey, pine	grapefruit, orange, honey with a good malt balance; finishes bitter with medium-rich mouthfeel

• tasters, pints, and flights available

COFOUNDERS JEFF TREVASKIS AND GARRY PITMAN want their lineup to offer something to the mainstream craft beer lover as well as the less-traditional types. A tasty Kolsch-style blonde, a red ale, a brown ale, a pale ale, and an IPA form the Manzanita core, but there are always other interesting additions, such as a smoky Rausch-style, a big double IPA, a tasty Kentucky Common sour beer, and—come October—one of San Diego's best pumpkin ales.

MISSION BREWERY (Downtown)

missionbrewery.com

3

1441 L St.
San Diego, CA 92101
(619) 544-0555

Mon–Fri: 12 pm–8 pm
Sat: 12 pm–10 pm
Sun: 12 pm–7 pm

IN TERMS OF SPACES TO TASTE BEER in San Diego, Mission Brewery ranks as one of the best. Housed inside the old Wonder Bread factory downtown, the exposed brick and vaulted 30-foot ceilings with skylights are the perfect setting for the super-long bar, shuffleboard table, and the very generous seating within.

If you have the inclination, you can wander around the brewhouse, bottling room, and fermentation tanks that fill the non-tasting areas of the brewery. When the place is jumping (like before and after Padres games) it can be loud, but there are plenty of areas within the space to find relative quiet, if desired.

tasting room	yes
beers on tap	12
cask / nitro	cask
tours	fri, sat & sun
kegs	5 & 15.5 gal.
growlers	64 oz.
bottles	22 oz.
six packs	yes
merchandise	yes
kid friendly	yes
dog friendly	yes
seating	generous
food	weekend food trucks

BEER	COLOR	AROMA	TASTE	
el conquistador 4.8% (extra pale ale)	light golden yellow	light notes of honey and hops with light malt	crisp and lightly malty with pleasing bitter finish	●●
mission hefeweizen 5.3%	hazy bright banana yellow	bready esters, clove, spice	spice, biscuit, banana, crisp and refreshing with light mouthfeel	●●
mission amber 5%	deep copper	light malt and caramel	crisp hoppiness balanced by light caramel malt	●●
shipwrecked 9.25% (double IPA)	deep golden copper yellow	floral pine, citrus, honey hops	citrus balanced by medium maltiness and nice bitter finish	●●
dark seas 9.8% (stout)	deep, dark brown	roasted chocolate, vanilla, malt	chocolate and malt with a creamy, rich mouthfeel; finishes with a touch of bitter and then sweetness	●●

• pints and flights available

COMPARED TO MOST OTHER BREWERIES of their size, Mission's lineup is fairly focused and streamlined, and in a good way. If you're a hef lover, you won't be disappointed by their Hefeweizen, or any of John Egan's other beers, which are solid takes on classic American-English styles that deliver satisfying flavor as well as good drinkability.

MODERN TIMES BEER (Point Loma)

moderntimesbeer.com 3

3725 Greenwood St.
San Diego, CA
92110

(323) 620-1136

Every day: 12 pm–9 pm

WHEN MODERN TIMES OPENED its doors in July 2013—in a factory-centric area of Point Loma—it expanded the reach of craft breweries into this part of town.

The spacious brewery and tasting room area, which together comprise more than 12,000 square feet, are adorned with a number of unique and interesting elements, including hundreds of volumes of old books, two very cool state-of-the-art growler fillers (no foam!), and an awesome mural from artist Amy Krone that is made from more than 12,000 Post-It notes.

tasting room	yes
beers on tap	16
cask / nitro	nitro
tours	by request
kegs	5 & 15.5 gal.
growlers	64 oz.
bottles	no
six packs	four pack cans
merchandise	yes
kid friendly	no
dog friendly	no
seating	limited
food	nearby

BEER	COLOR	AROMA	TASTE
lomaland saison 5.5%	medium yellow with a slight haze	clove, banana, spice with light bready esters	spice, clove, hints of orange peel, crisp and clean
fortunate islands hoppy wheat 4.8%	medium golden yellow	citrus and floral with hints of bready yeasts	pine, floral, and citrus; clean and crisp with a mostly bitter finish
blazing world amber IPA 6.8%	medium amber	pine, citrus, and floral hoppiness	caramel and toffee balanced by crisp citrus, pine, and floral hops with a mostly bitter finish
black house oatmeal coffee stout 5.8%	deep black	coffee, chocolate, caramel, and vanilla	coffee, roasty malt, chocolate; medium bodied with a mostly dry finish
neverwhere brett trois IPA 7%	hazy golden yellow	mango, pineapple, citrus	honey, lemon, bread and hay; light bodied, crisp and clean

- tasters, pints, and flights available

HEAD BREWER DEREK FREESE has developed a unique and creative lineup of well-balanced beers that include interesting (and well-done) variations on classic styles, such as his hoppy wheat beer, his amber IPA, and his Brett trois IPA. Also of note: the coffee for the oatmeal coffee stout is roasted right there at the brewery.

MONKEY PAW PUB & BREWERY (East Village)

monkeypaw
brewing.com

3

805 16th St.
San Diego, CA 92101
(619) 358-9901

Mon–Thur: 12 pm–11:59 pm
Fri–Sun: 12pm–2 am

LIKE ITS FOUNDER, CRAFT-BEER-BAR PIONEER Scot Blair, Monkey Paw is one of a kind. There are one or two other bars in town that also brew beer on site, but Monkey Paw is a real working boutique brewery that brews more than 40 styles of beer and usually has at least 8 to 12 of them on tap at the bar.

The bar is a comfortable, neighborhood place, covered in dark work and brick, which offers a large selection of beers in bottles as well as on tap. Monkey Paw is not a brewpub, but rather it's a bar with a brewery attached. The kitchen produces particularly delicious and satisfying bar food (get

tasting room	bar
beers on tap	31+
cask / nitro	cask
tours	no
kegs	no
growlers	64 oz.
bottles	no
six packs	cans
merchandise	yes
kid friendly	no
dog friendly	no
seating	very good
food	full menu

BEER	COLOR	AROMA	TASTE
sweet georgia brown 5%	deep copper brown	chocolate, caramel malt, vanilla, caramel	chocolate, caramel, malt with crispness and medium mouthfeel
low and slow 5.4% (rauchbier)	golden yellow amber	smoky bacon and floral hops	smoked bacon balanced by crisp floral hop notes
hooked on chinook 5.2% (single hop IPA)	medium dark golden yellow	grapefruit, earthy, spice	crisp grapfruit and floral spiciness, clean and crisp
bonobos 5.6% (San Diego pale ale)	light golden yellow	sweet citrus and honey hops	citrus, floral, honey, medium mouthfeel
kong 11.8% (barleywine)	deep copper	honey, raisin, toffee, bread	raisin, dried fruit, toffee, caramel with a nice crisp hoppy finish

• tasters, pints, and flights available

one of the 4 kinds of cheesesteaks!) that includes salads, corned beef sandwiches, wings, and 4 kinds of fries.

SCOT HAS RECENTLY TAKEN ON Cosimo Sorrentino as Monkey Paw's head brewer and the results are outstanding. Interesting specialty and seasonal beers are always in rotation, and Scot and Cosimo are constantly searching for creative new flavor combinations and stylistic twists, such as their amazing Great Ape Nectar (hazelnut milk stout) and their Valentine's Ale (which tastes like gingerbread in a glass).

MOTHER EARTH BREW COMPANY (Vista)

motherearth
brewco.com
206 Main St., Vista, CA 92084
(760) 726-2273
Mon: Closed
Tue, Wed: 12 pm–8 pm
Thur: 12 pm–10 pm
Fri, Sat: 12 pm–11 pm
Sun: 12 pm–9 pm

1

MOTHER EARTH BREW COMPANY is one of North County's brightest brewing success stories. First opened in 2010 as a combination homebrew supply shop and brewery, the company quickly won loyal fans and followers with its wide variety of quality beers.

The original homebrew space, now expanded, still operates as the brewery (with a tasting area), but the primary venue for Mother Earth is their tap house in downtown Vista. This large, mostly open indoor space features a big bar, a selection of big tables and stools, and a small outdoor patio.

tasting room	yes
beers on tap	10
cask / nitro	yes
tours	no
kegs	no
growlers	1 & 2 liter
bottles	22 oz.
six packs	no
merchandise	yes
kid friendly	yes
dog friendly	yes
seating	very good
food	nearby

BEER	COLOR	AROMA	TASTE
cali cream ale 5.2%	medium golden yellow	vanilla, biscuits and bread	vanilla, maltiness; rich mouthfeel balanced by light, crisp, slightly sweet finish
double decker English brown ale 5.2%	deep amber orange	roasted coffee, caramel	big malty coffee, with nutty notes; crisp, light mouthfeel; finishes dry
blonde siren 5.4%	golden yellow	malty, biscuit with citrus notes	lightly malty, crisp and clean, with light mouthfeel and bitter finish
pin up pale ale 5.6%	hazy amber orange	pine, lemon, grapefruit	lemon, citrus, grapefruit, hints of pine; bitter finish with trailing slight sweetness
red dog rye IPA 5.7%	medium golden yellow	big citrus, lemon, grass, pine with malty notes	lemon, citrus, grapefruit with medium mouthfeel, bitter finish with slightly sweet end note
kismet IPA 7.2%	amber copper	grassy, hints of white wine	big citrus and lemon, with notes of wet grass; crisp with balanced bitterness

• tasters, half pints, pints, and flights available

OWNER-BREWER DAN LOVE is a talented and fun-loving brewer—an outgoing guy who doesn't take himself too seriously. He likes to brew a wide range of styles and likes to play with them as well (his bourbon-barrel-aged peanut butter stout is just one example). In addition to his more esoteric recipes, Dan also brews a number of highly aromatic, full-flavored, hoppy ales that come in below 6% ABV and deliver great drinkability without the high octane.

Other locations:
2055 Thibodo Rd., Vista, CA 92081
(760) 599-4225

For homebrew supplies and tasting:
Mon–Wed: Closed; Thur: 4 pm–8 pm;
Fri: 4 pm–9 pm; Sat: 12 pm–7 pm;
Sun: 12 pm–6 pm

NEW ENGLISH BREWING COMPANY (Sorrento Valley)

newenglish
brewing.com
11545 Sorrento Valley Rd.
Suite 305
San Diego, CA 92121
(619) 857-8023
Sun–Wed: Closed
Thur, Fri: 4 pm–7 pm
Sat: 2 pm–6 pm

2

THE RECENT MOVE AND EXPANSION of New English is a testament to the fact that the company has gained a lot of fans in recent years. New English has been brewing in San Diego since 2008, and has gained a reputation as a solid and well-respected member of the brewing community.

The new brewery and tasting room space occupies a corner in a large office park complex. A small bar sits among the brewing equipment and bottling machine, where visitors can stand and sip as they look over the operation.

tasting room	yes
beers on tap	8
cask / nitro	cask
tours	no
kegs	no
growlers	64 oz.
bottles	22 oz.
six packs	no
merchandise	yes
kid friendly	yes
dog friendly	yes
seating	no
food	nearby

BEER	COLOR	AROMA	TASTE
troopers tipple IPA 5.1%	golden yellow	grassy, floral hops, hints of citrus	mellow honey hops, light maltiness, balanced, medium mouthfeel
explorer esb 5.8%	amber-copper red	toffee, caramel, biscuit	rich malt caramel, toffee, low bitterness with slightly sweet finish
brewers special brown 6.6%	dark brownish copper	caramel malt, toffee, hints of roasted coffee	chocolate, coffee malt, medium mouthfeel, finishes slightly sweet
dragoon red 6.9%	deep copper	malt and toffee balanced with floral hops	caramel, toffee malts balanced with crisp, clean hops and clean finish
pacific storm stout 5% (dry Irish stout)	dark, inky black	coffee, chocolate, vanilla	chocolate and coffee well balanced with bitterness, medium mouthfeel, finishes dry

• tasters, pints, and flights available

FOUNDER AND BREWER SIMON LACEY has created a quality lineup that focuses on putting a "West Coast spin" on traditional English styles. As a result, New English offers a few more malt-forward brews than most, and tends to work with a more subdued approach to hops. The tasting room is equipped with two casks, which provide extra dimension to many beers, especially the Dragoon Red, which was exceptional on cask.

OCEANSIDE ALE WORKS (Oceanside)

oceansidealeworks.net 1

1800 Ord Way
Oceanside, CA 92056
(760) 721-4253

Mon–Wed: Closed
Thur, Fri: 3 pm–8 pm
Sat, Sun: 12 pm–6 pm

BECAUSE IT'S HIDDEN INSIDE a nondescript concrete corporate office park, walking into Oceanside Ale Works feels a little like you've stumbled upon a beer Shangri-la. A large, high-ceilinged brewery and tasting space provide a lively airplane hangar–type setting that offers a few booths, a long bar, and a variety of bar tables and barrels for standing and sipping.

Brewers Ryan Hamill and Jake Whyte know what they're doing—and they've been doing it well for a while. Oceanside Ale Works, which was Oceanside's first brewery, has been part of the San Diego craft beer scene since 2006, and their fan base is both large and loyal.

tasting room	yes
beers on tap	10
cask / nitro	cask
tours	by request
kegs	5 & 15.5 gal.
growlers	64 oz.
bottles	22 oz.
six packs	no
merchandise	yes
kid friendly	yes
dog friendly	no
seating	good
food	thur–sun food tents

BEER	COLOR	AROMA	TASTE	
buccaneer blonde 5%	light golden yellow	European malt with light hop notes	lightly malty, crisp, with a slightly sweet and balanced finish	●●
san luis rey red 5.8%	medium amber copper	caramel malts with hints of coffee and toffee	caramel maltiness with hints of honey; crisp but with rich creamy mouthfeel	●●
pirate's cove IPA 6.8%	medium golden	citrus hops, grass	citrus, grass, with notes of white pepper; crisp with bitter finish	●
elevation 83 extreme pale ale 8.3%	medium amber copper	caramel, toffee, with piney and citrus hops	citrus flavors first, followed by malty caramel; finishes bitter with slight sweetness	●
American strong ale 9.2%	amber orange copper	big malty caramel with vanilla notes	big caramel and toffee with rich mouthfeel; finishes bitter with slight sweetness	●●

• tasters, pints, and flights available

THE BEER LINEUP offers something for nearly every taste, everything from their outstanding crisp blonde ale to their big, rich, and malty American strong ale.

OFFBEAT BREWING COMPANY (Escondido)

offbeatbrewing.com
1223 Pacific Oaks Pl.
Escondido, CA 92029
(760) 294-4045
Mon, Tue: Closed
Wed, Thur: 3 pm–8 pm
Fri: 3 pm–9 pm
Sat: 12 pm–8 pm
Sun: 12 pm–7 pm

1

IN SEPTEMBER 2012, FORMER STONE Brewing Co. brewer, Tom Garcia, went out on his own. But he didn't go far. He and his wife, Sarah, opened Offbeat Brewing Company about a quarter mile down the road—only a "stone's throw" away.

The office park that houses Offbeat is typical-looking on the outside, but rather funky and whimsical on the inside. Here, extra-high ceilings with large walls of windows provide a pleasing and airy environment in which to stand and sip. Also notable is the unique and interesting artwork from local artists that adorn the walls—the most impressive of which is a huge contemporary mural that covers a wall high above the tasting room.

tasting room	yes
beers on tap	6
cask / nitro	cask
tours	no
kegs	15.5 gal.
growlers	64 oz.
bottles	no
six packs	no
merchandise	yes
kid friendly	yes
dog friendly	yes
seating	some
food	no

BEER	COLOR	AROMA	TASTE
deer grandpa abbey dubbel 6.6%	copper brown	tropical fruit with biscuit maltiness and citrus notes	toffee malt with dry fruit, raisins, tropical fruit; medium mouthfeel with a nutty, bitter finish
caticom IPA 7.7%	dark rust orange	honey and apricot	caramel malt with notes of citrus and honey; finishes bitter
grain-fed dog 8% (American strong ale)	dark amber copper	dry fruit, bready esters	roasted malt, notes of tropical fruit and bubble gum; medium mouthfeel balanced with a bitter finish

• tasters, pints, and flights available

TOM MAY BE A former brewer for Stone, but the beers he is making are not the big hop-bombs many people expect. Tom and Sarah are particularly fond of more malt-forward beers, and their solid lineup of well-balanced but malt-centric brews reflects that.

OGGI'S PIZZA & BREWING COMPANY (Mission Valley)

missionvalley
.oggis.com

2

2245 Fenton Pkwy.
San Diego, CA 92108
(619) 640-1072

Mon–Fri: 11 am–10 pm
Sat, Sun: 9 am–12 am

TUCKED INTO A LARGE MALL NEAR Qualcomm Stadium, Oggi's is a welcoming, family-friendly, pizza-centric restaurant and sports bar that also offers beer brewed on the premises.

Visitors can sit at the medium-sized bar, or at booths, bar tables, or an outdoor patio. More than two dozen hi-def flat screen TVs offer coverage of major sporting events, and a full bar has plenty of options for non-beer-drinkers.

tasting room	bar / restaurant
beers on tap	11 house / 1 guest
cask / nitro	cask
tours	by request
kegs	no
growlers	64 oz.
bottles	no
six packs	no
merchandise	yes
kid friendly	yes
dog friendly	outside patio
seating	good
food	full menu

BEER	COLOR	AROMA	TASTE
McGarvey's Scottish ale 5.2%	medium brown	caramel malt, hints of nuttiness	caramel with tropical notes, light mouthfeel with a slightly sweet finish
torrey pines IPA 6.8%	medium golden	honey, pine, light citrus	citrus hops, light mouthfeel with mostly bitter finish
black magic stout 7.8%	deep dark brown	roasted coffee and caramel	roasted coffee, chocolate maltiness with light mouthfeel
presidio double IPA 8.5%	medium orange	floral and citrus hops	honey, citrus, and floral hoppiness with a clean, bitter finish

• tasters, pints, 21 oz. mugs, pitchers, and flights available

BREWER JOHN WILSON keeps a steady lineup of 11 beers on tap, which include about 7 or 8 core brews and then some seasonals. The beers are designed to pair well with simple brewpub-type fare, and most offerings are very straightforward.

OGGI'S PIZZA & BREWING COMPANY (Carmel Mountain)

cmr.oggis.com

10155 Rancho
Carmel Dr.
San Diego, CA 92128

(858) 592-7883

Every day: 11 am–10 pm

THROUGH THE YEARS, A NUMBER of excellent brewers have cycled through Oggi's, at various locations. Unlike many of its counterparts, this franchise has historically been fairly serious about providing good quality beer alongside its pizza-centric, family-friendly menu. Today, only two Oggi's remain in San Diego, and they are now operated by separate owners.

The large, comfortable space in Carmel Mountain can host parties of any kind. There are booths and big tables for families, bar tables for couples, and plenty of space at the bar if you're on your own. Flat-screen TVs surround you, all tuned to one sports channel or another.

tasting room	bar / restaurant
beers on tap	9 house / 5 guest
cask / nitro	yes
tours	no
kegs	no
growlers	64 oz.
bottles	no
six packs	no
merchandise	yes
kid friendly	yes
dog friendly	no
seating	very good
food	full menu

BEER	COLOR	AROMA	TASTE
cali gold 4.8% (blonde ale)	light gold	light bready malt	light malt with medium mouthfeel and slightly sweet finish
sweet spot hefeweizen 5.2%	hazy light golden yellow	clove, spice,and yeasty esters with hints of banana	clove with hints of banana and black pepper; light and crisp
surfside monk 8.9% (Belgian Tripel)	golden yellow with a slight haze	clove, honey, yeasty esters	clove, honey, with hints of biscuit
McGarvey's Scottish ale 5.2%	dark amber	caramel toffee, hint of butterscotch	caramel and toffee with vanilla notes; creamy mouthfeel with slightly sweet finish
torrey pines IPA 6.8%	medium golden orange	light hints of citrus	lemon notes with a bitter finish

• tasters, pints, 21 oz. mugs, pitchers, and flights available

THE BEER LINEUP AT THIS OGGI'S IS BREWED by two separate entities. On site, brewer Eric Loper does a rotation of three beers, which can include Belgian styles and wheat beers. The rest of the beer is contract-brewed by Left Coast Brewing in San Clemente.

ON-THE-TRACKS BREWERY (Carlsbad)

ottbrew.com
5674 El Camino Real
Carlsbad, CA 92008
(760) 550-9688
Mon–Wed: Closed
Thur: 4 pm–8 pm
Fri: 4 pm–9 pm
Sat: 1 pm–9 pm
Sun: 1 pm–4:30 pm

1

SINCE IT OPENED A FEW YEARS BACK, On-The-Tracks has focused on brewing mostly English- and Scottish-style beers. The family-owned-and-operated brewery works on a small system and produces a relatively small quantity of beer that is not widely distributed around San Diego.

A small suite in an office park houses the tasting room, which is separated from the brewing area and equipment. The tasting space is small, spare, and simple, with only a few stools and not much to look at.

tasting room	yes
beers on tap	14
cask / nitro	nitro
tours	by request
kegs	5 gallon
growlers	yes
bottles	22 oz.
six packs	no
merchandise	yes
kid friendly	yes
dog friendly	yes
seating	limited
food	summer food trucks

BEER	COLOR	AROMA	TASTE
ginger beer 4.0%	light golden yellow	light malt	light, crisp, hint of eucalyptus
baltic pepper porter 8.0%	deep, dark brown	roasted malt, hint of smoke	roasted malt, smokiness, mild pepper heat
old bastard ale 6.5%	deep reddish brown	faint	light, faint hops
golden spike 6.0%	light reddish gold	faint	hints of sweet malt
sour spike 5.0%	deep, dark brown	sour berry	sour fruit with floral hops

- tasters, half pints, pints, and flights available

PACIFIC BEACH ALE HOUSE (Pacific Beach)

pbalehouse.com

721 Grand Ave.
San Diego, CA 92109

(858) 581-2337

Mon–Fri: 11 am–2 am
Sat, Sun: 9 am–2 am

2

IF YOU HEAD WEST ON GRAND AVENUE as far as you can go, your journey will end at the beach, and at Pacific Beach Ale House. There, you'll find a friendly neighborhood brewpub that offers patrons nourishment after a tiring day playing in the sand and surf.

The large space—adorned with stone and wood of all types—offers seating options of all kinds, including booths, tables, bar seating, an outdoor patio, and a terrace that provides the best view of the water. A full menu, which includes flat breads, sandwiches, ribs, and tacos (among many other things), offers something for nearly every taste.

tasting room	bar / restaurant
beers on tap	9 house / 5 guest
cask / nitro	nitro
tours	no
kegs	no
growlers	64 oz.
bottles	no
six packs	no
merchandise	yes
kid friendly	yes
dog friendly	outside patio
seating	plenty
food	full menu

BEER	COLOR	AROMA	TASTE
good times gold 4.25%	light yellow	light malt with hints of bread	light, crisp maltiness
crystal pier pale ale 5.5%	medium orange	light caramel malt	light malty caramel, slightly sweet with a bitter finish
promiscuous IPA 7%	light amber orange	light notes of citrus and honey	light honey and citrus, with crisp and bitter finish
double IPA 8.1%	medium amber orange	light notes of citrus and honey	light maltiness with hints of wood
mango wheat 6%	hazy apricot	bready, malty esters; tropical fruit with a hint of orange-mango	bready yeastiness, citrus, honey with a light mouthfeel

• tasters, half pints, pints, 22 oz. mugs, and flights available

THE STRAIGHTFORWARD CORE BEER lineup at PB Ale House is designed to pair well with all kinds of food and is built around the basic styles that most patrons request while dining. Most selections are easy to drink and work well for this kind of pub-like setting.

PIZZA PORT CARLSBAD (Carlsbad)

pizzaport.com

571 Carlsbad Village Dr.
Carlsbad, CA 92008

(760) 720-7007

Sun–Thur: 11 am–10 pm
Fri, Sat: 11 am–12 am

1

BROTHER-AND-SISTER TEAM Vince and Gina Marsaglia have built their Pizza Port business into one of San Diego's premier craft beer franchises. Their model? Make truly great beer (more major awards than any other San Diego brewery) and serve it with simple food in a fun, relaxed, and family-friendly atmosphere.

Of course, Pizza Port's great success and popularity means it's often jammed with locals, regulars, and beer pilgrims. This Carlsbad location, which is the second-largest of the group, offers long, family-style tables—both inside and out—where groups can socialize around pizza and pitchers.

tasting room	bar / restaurant
beers on tap	24+
cask / nitro	yes
tours	no
kegs	no
growlers	yes
bottles	no
six packs	no
merchandise	yes
kid friendly	yes
dog friendly	no
seating	very good
food	pizza, salad & wings

BEER	COLOR	AROMA	TASTE
grandview golden ale 7%	medium golden yellow	light malt, floral hops	crisp hops, light, honey malt tones
shark bite red 6.5%	reddish golden amber	caramel, toffee malt notes with floral hops	caramel malt balanced with crisp hop crispness and medium bitterness
silky heads lemongrass wheat 4.7%	light straw yellow, touch of haze	floral hops, lemongrass	light, crisp, lemongrass and hop flavors: drinks more ale than wheat
seaside stout 5.3%	deep, dark brown	roasty malt, hints of chocolate	bitter chocolate, coffee, medium body finishes dry

• tasters, half pints, pints, pitchers, and flights available

It's not a quiet night out, but it is a friendly, boisterous, and happy scene.

A WIDE VARIETY OF BEERS rotate through each Pizza Port location, many of which are brewed on site and many of which are handpicked guest beers. No matter what's up on the board, beer fans of all kinds are sure to find something delicious that will satisfy any taste.

PIZZA PORT BRESSI RANCH (Carlsbad)

www.pizzaport.com

2730 Gateway Rd.
Carlsbad, CA 92009

(760) 707-1655

Sun–Thur: 11 am-10 pm
Fri, Sat: 11 am-11 pm

1

THE LARGEST PIZZA PORT to open thus far, this impressive brand-new facility (opened summer of 2013) offers fans two stories of ample indoor eating and drinking space, a spacious and comfortable outdoor lounge, a full menu of food and beers, all wrapped up in the casual, low-key surfer-inspired package that has pleased Pizza Port fans for years. Visitors can glimpse inside the huge brewing facility that's housed next door, where Pizza Port has expanded its production considerably.

tasting room	bar / restaurant
beers on tap	24+
cask / nitro	yes
tours	no
kegs	no
growlers	yes
bottles	no
six packs	no
merchandise	yes
kid friendly	yes
dog friendly	outside patio
seating	very good
food	pizza, salad & wings

PIZZA PORT OCEAN BEACH (Ocean Beach)

pizzaport.com

3

1956 Bacon St.
San Diego, CA 92107

(619) 224-4700

Sun–Thur: 11 am–10 pm
Fri, Sat: 11 am–12 am

JUST LIKE ITS SISTER locations around the county, this Pizza Port offers a hard-to-beat combination of surf, sand, great beer, and great food. Laid-back, family friendly, and always pouring an excellent selection of all styles, this is the place to come if you want to experience a true "San Diego Beer/Surfer" vibe.

tasting room	bar / restaurant
beers on tap	24+
cask / nitro	yes
tours	no
kegs	no
growlers	yes
bottles	no
six packs	no
merchandise	yes
kid friendly	yes
dog friendly	outside patio
seating	very good
food	pizza, salad & wings

PIZZA PORT SOLANA BEACH (Solana Beach)

pizzaport.com

135 N Hwy. 101
Solana Beach, CA 92075

(858) 481-7332

Sun–Thur: 11 am–10 pm
Fri, Sat: 11 am–12 am

1

LIKE ITS CARLSBAD AND OCEAN BEACH brethren, Pizza Port Solana Beach is all about having a great place to hang out with friends or family, preferably after a great day at the beach. The comfortable, no-frills, friendly surroundings belie the fact that Pizza Port beers are some of the best and most highly decorated brews in San Diego.

Big, long wooden picnic-style tables fill the main space, along with smaller tables, benches, and stools. An outdoor seating area offers an additional option for those who prefer fresh air. Arcade machines, flat screens, and serve-yourself paper plates all contribute to an energetic but casual atmosphere where people are as comfortable in flip-flops and bathing suits as anything else.

NO-NONSENSE, STRAIGHTFORWARD American styles with great flavors are the backbone of the Pizza Port lineup. A wide variety of beers are in rotation at each location, so you'll have to check the colorful hand-lettered signs above the bar to see what's on tap each day. Luckily, no matter what's on tap, it's bound to be good.

tasting room	bar / restaurant
beers on tap	24+
cask / nitro	yes
tours	no
kegs	no
growlers	yes
bottles	no
six packs	no
merchandise	yes
kid friendly	yes
dog friendly	outside patio
seating	very good
food	pizza, salad & wings

POOR HOUSE BREWING CO. (North Park)

poorhousebrew.com

3

4494 30th St.
San Diego, CA 92116

(858) 769-9070

Every day: 2 pm–12 am

THIS BAR AND TINY BREW operation opened its doors in 2012, in the bustling craft-beer-centric community of North Park. More bar than brewery, the small, dimly lit space houses the requisite pool table, uses chalkboard signage, offers peanuts and pretzels, and serves its homebrews in glass Ball jars.

The Poor House brews are predominantly IPAs and Belgian-style ales of various strengths and hoppiness. On average, the bar offers 4 or 5 Poor House beers, along with guest taps and bottled selections.

tasting room	bar
beers on tap	9+
cask / nitro	no
tours	no
kegs	no
growlers	no
bottles	no
six packs	no
merchandise	yes
kid friendly	no
dog friendly	no
seating	bar
food	pizza

BEER	COLOR	AROMA	TASTE
IPA experimental batch 6 6.8%	deep golden yellow	citrus notes	crisp, hoppy, well balanced
Belgian ale 8.1%	golden yellow	faint yeastiness	light mouthfeel
American strong ale 7.7%	dark amber copper	light maltiness, hops	mix of roastiness, hops, and light malts
my bitter side IPA 8.7%	dark golden	faint hops	light hops, light mouthfeel

• tasters, pints, and flights available

* cash only

PORT BREWING / THE LOST ABBEY (San Marcos)

lostabbey.com
155 Mata Way, #104
San Marcos, CA 92069
(800) 918-6816
Mon, Tue: 1 pm–6 pm
Wed: 1 pm–9 pm
Thur: 1 pm–7 pm
Fri: 1 pm–9 pm
Sat: 11:30 am–8 pm
Sun: 12 pm–7 pm

1

MUCH OF THE PORT/LOST ABBEY brewery is festooned with ornaments and images that evoke a Belgian abbey. The religious-flavored vibe (all done in good fun) is apt, because Lost Abbey is, in fact, almost a holy site for people who love serious Belgian-inspired beers.

The tasting room space can be a bit dark with few places to sit, but it is plenty large enough to accommodate the many fans who swarm there daily. A separate barrel room behind the bar area provides a quieter, unique space in which to stand, talk, and taste.

tasting room	yes
beers on tap	18+
cask / nitro	no
tours	weekends
kegs	no
growlers	64 oz.
bottles	22 oz., 375 & 750 ml.
six packs	no
merchandise	yes
kid friendly	yes
dog friendly	no
seating	no
food	wed–sun food truck

BEER	COLOR	AROMA	TASTE
road to helles 5.2%	golden yellow	light malt, floral hops, with bready, honey notes	light crisp malt with notes of biscuits and honey
avant garde 7% (bier de garde)	orange copper gold	light, bready malt with notes of orange and floral hops	light, crisp, with orange and citrus; finishes mostly bitter with slight sweetness
red barn 6.8% (saison)	hazy golden yellow	bready esters with citrus and ginger notes	light and crisp with yeasty, bready esters and orange peel, black pepper, and ginger notes
judgment day 10.5% (abbey quad)	deep copper reddish brown	raisins, dry fruit, molasses	deep bready esters with notes of dry fruit and molasses; rich mouthfeel
mongo 8% (double IPA)	golden orange	big lemon and citrus hops	big citrus and honey balanced by crisp bitter hoppiness; finishes bitter with a hint of sweet
shark attack 9.5% (double red)	amber copper	caramel and toffee malt	citrus hops balanced with rich caramel malt; medium mouthfeel with a slightly sweet finish

- tasters, half pints, and pints available

LEGENDARY BREWER

Tomme Arthur oversees both the Port line and the Lost Abbey line. The Port beers are, without exception, all great takes on classic American/West Coast brews that deliver big, satisfying flavor in a wide range of styles. Though many fans flock for their hoppy IPAs, Port's darker beers (such as Old Viscosity and Board Meeting) are also delicious. The Belgian-inspired beers of Lost Abbey also shine, and have become the gold standard for all other San Diego brewers who aspire to that style. Lost Abbey has an extensive barrel-aging program, which produces incredible beers, some of which are unparalleled anywhere in the world.

PROHIBITION BREWING COMPANY (Vista)

prohibitionbrewing company.com

2004 E. Vista Way
Vista, CA 92084

(760) 295-3525

Every day: 11 am–11 pm

1

IN 2011, PROHIBITION STARTED BREWING on a small system in the northernmost reaches of San Diego County. In 2013, they expanded the operation with a brand-new 10-barrel brewhouse.

The brewing equipment is tucked away in the back area of Prohibition's brewpub, which offers a large, dimly lit family-friendly space with big tables and plenty of room. Visitors can order from a full menu that includes burgers, sandwiches, ribs, steaks, tacos, nachos, and salads.

tasting room	bar / restaurant
beers on tap	8 house / 16 guest
cask / nitro	nitro
tours	no
kegs	5 & 15.5 gal.
growlers	64 oz.
bottles	no
six packs	no
merchandise	yes
kid friendly	yes
dog friendly	no
seating	very good
food	full menu

BEER	COLOR	AROMA	TASTE
shotgun saison 5%	light yellow	light malt	hints of malt, esters; crisp
extra pale ale 5.2%	medium golden yellow	light malt	light malt, notes of caramel; finishes slightly sweet with low bitterness
ruby red ale 6.2%	medium amber	light caramel malts	caramel with hints of roasted coffee; finishes slightly sweet
dirty blonde 6.3%	golden yellow	light malt	light malt with estery notes
hef u up 8.%	clear, medium golden yellow	light malt with hints of honey	light malt, honey, bread with slightly sweet finish and low bitterness

• tasters, half pints, pints, and flights available

THE BEER lineup encompasses a number of mostly light styles that include a blonde, a hef, a saison, and a pale ale.

RIP CURRENT BREWING CO. (San Marcos)

ripcurrentbrewing.com
1325 Grand Ave.
Suite 100
San Marcos, CA 92078
(760) 481-3141
Mon, Tue: Closed
Wed, Thur: 5 pm–8 pm
Fri: 4 pm–9 pm
Sat: 12 pm–9 pm
Sun: 12 pm–5 pm

1

BY THE TIME RIP CURRENT OPENED its doors at the end of 2012, its debut had been much anticipated for quite some time. Co-founders Paul Sangster and Guy Shobe have well-established and highly respected track records as homebrewers—in fact, Sangster won the 2011 Ninkasi award from the American Homebrewers Association, essentially bestowing upon him the title of Best Homebrewer in America.

The Rip Current tasting room is an airy, light-filled space with a smallish bar, beer barrel tables, and a decent number of seats. It's a refreshing change from the usual dark, mostly windowless spaces that characterize many brewery tasting rooms.

tasting room	yes
beers on tap	9+
cask / nitro	yes
tours	by request
kegs	5 gal
growlers	yes
bottles	no
six packs	no
merchandise	yes
kid friendly	yes
dog friendly	yes
seating	fair
food	food trucks

BEER	COLOR	AROMA	TASTE
barrier reef nut brown 5%	dark brown, caramel	caramel malt	crisp, light refreshing malt with hints of hazelnut and bitter chocolate
tube rye-der IPA 5.3%	light, golden	sweet honey hops	hoppy with sweet honey and tropical notes; lighter bodied but very flavorful
raked over red 6.%	dark reddish amber	malty, caramel	light, toasty malt
lupilin lust IPA 8.2%	golden yellow	wheaty, sweet honey	round, mellow hoppiness, lightly sweet
rescue buoy Russian imperial stout 11.2%	dark, deep molasses brown	brown sugar, honey, oatmeal	dark fruit, brown bread, molasses

• tasters, 13 oz. tulips, pints, and flights available

MUCH OF SANGSTER and Shobe's initial lineup concentrates on variations of classic American styles, all well done and easy to drink. Of particular note is the Tube Rye-Der IPA, which—at only 5.3% ABV—is a full-flavored, satisfying, very sessionable IPA that doesn't sacrifice flavor for drinkability.

ROCK BOTTOM BREWERY RESTAURANT (GASLAMP)

rockbottom.com/san-diego

3

401 G St.
San Diego, CA 92101
(619) 231-7000

Sun–Thur: 11 am–12 am
Fri, Sat: 11 am–2 am

EVEN WITH THE BOOM IN SAN DIEGO craft beer, there are still relatively few breweries actually making beer downtown. Luckily, Rock Bottom is one of them. Located right in the heart of San Diego's Gaslamp District, this brewery restaurant offers patrons plenty of space, a large bar, and a full menu in addition to a nice variety of handcrafted brews.

Head brewer Jason Stockberger is a skilled artisan who combines talent with a youthful exuberance and a love of craft beer. His regular lineup includes beers from a variety of classic styles, including light, refreshing German hefs and Kolsch ales, American reds and IPAs, stouts, and a few

tasting room	bar / restaurant
beers on tap	10
cask / nitro	yes
tours	by request
kegs	5 & 15.5 gal.
growlers	64 oz.
bottles	no
six packs	no
merchandise	yes
kid friendly	yes
dog friendly	outside patio
seating	very good
food	full menu

BEER	COLOR	AROMA	TASTE	
Belgian style white ale 5%	hazy, light golden yellow	bready esters, orange peel, clove	clove, spice, light and crisp with light malt finish	●
angry dragon imperial IPA 8.9%	deep orange	orange peel, citrus, floral hops	honey, floral notes, medium maltiness, finishes with malty bitterness and touch of sweet	●●
rock bottom brown ale 4.9%	deep copper brown	malty caramel and toffee	medium caramel maltiness with crisp medium mouthfeel, mostly dry finish	●●
sunset stout 5.3%	deep, dark brown	chocolate, vanilla, coffee	chocolate with roasted coffee, creamy mouthfeel, finishes semi-sweet	●
bourbon barrel aged red 6.25%	deep copper red	bourbon, caramel, vanilla, toffee	rich, boozy bourbon with chocolate, vanilla, and toffee; medium mouthfeel	●●

• tasters, half pints, pints, and flights available

Belgian-style ales. Depending on when you stop in, Jason will likely have one of his small-batch bourbon-barrel-aged beers available (he mostly does reds, browns, IPAs, and stouts)—they are worth asking for, as is Jason's silver-medal brown ale, which is part of the core beer menu.

ROCK BOTTOM BREWERY RESTAURANT (La Jolla)

2

rockbottom.com/la-jolla
8980 Villa La Jolla Dr.
La Jolla, CA 92037
(858) 450-9277
Mon–Thur: 11 am–12 am
Fri: 11 am–1 am
Sat: 11:30 am–1 am
Sun: 11:30 am–12 am

AT ROCK BOTTOM, THE FOCUS has always been as much on the quality of the beer as it has been on the food. In San Diego, this focus is often a given, but it's always nice to see.

The restaurant is large and comfortable with a big bar and many options for seating. Scattered in among the tables and booths are the various components of the Rock Bottom brewing operation, which is mostly on display behind glass.

tasting room	bar / restaurant
beers on tap	10
cask / nitro	yes
tours	by request
kegs	5 & 15.5 gal.
growlers	64 oz.
bottles	no
six packs	no
merchandise	yes
kid friendly	yes
dog friendly	outside patio
seating	very good
food	full menu

BEER	COLOR	AROMA	TASTE
kolsch 5%	light straw	light, sweet malts	light, sweet maltiness, crisp and balanced with slight bitterness
white ale 5.3%	golden yellow	sweet honey malt with notes of coriander and orange	honey malt with notes of orange, coriander, and spice; slightly sour finish
ragtop red 5.7%	golden copper	caramel and toast	caramel and toffee nicely balanced with hoppy crispness; medium-bodied
IPA 6.5%	golden orange	citrus, grapefruit	citrus with honey notes and pleasing, mostly bitter finish

• tasters, half pints, pints, and flights available

AWARD-WINNING BREWMASTER Marty Mendiola uses his considerable brewing talents to create a range of core beers that tend to focus on classic American and English styles. Even though his beers are accessible and very food-friendly, they don't sacrifice complexity or flavor. If you have the chance, don't miss Rudolph's Red or Moonlight Porter, both of which have won multiple medals at national competitions.

ROUGH DRAFT BREWING COMPANY (Mira Mesa)

roughdraftbrew.com

2

8830 Recho Rd.
San Diego, CA 92121
(858) 453-7238
Mon, Tue: Closed
Wed–Fri: 3 pm–9 pm
Sat: 1 pm–7 pm
Sun: 1 pm–4 pm

ONE OF THE FIRST NEW BREWERIES to open its doors in 2012, Rough Draft entered the San Diego brewing fray with an admirable variety of beers and styles.

The spacious tasting room is filled with numerous options that range from standing at a big bar, to sitting at large comfortable tables, to lounging in a sofa and love-seat area. Rough Draft's impressive brewing equipment dominates the room, which also boasts high ceilings and good light.

tasting room	yes
beers on tap	12
cask / nitro	yes
tours	by request
kegs	5 & 15.5 gal.
growlers	32 & 64 oz.
bottles	22 oz.
six packs	no
merchandise	yes
kid friendly	no
dog friendly	yes
seating	good
food	weekend food trucks

BEER	COLOR	AROMA	TASTE
eraser IPA 7%	light golden yellow	honey, floral hops	medium floral and honey hops, light mouthfeel
Belgian blond 6.2%	light yellow, straw	Belgian yeastiness, light malt	light maltiness balanced by crisp hops
Belgian vanilla stout 5%	dark amber brown	roasted coffee, vanilla	vanilla, coffee, medium mouthfeel, finishes dry
barrel aged emboozlement 8.3% (trippel)	golden yellow	pineapple, tropical fruit	vanilla and pineapple, hints of bourbon and tropical fruit
hop therapy double IPA 9%	medium orange gold	faint topical hop	light hops with hints of honey, finishes medium bitter

• tasters, pints, and flights available

OWNER AND FOUNDER

Jeff Silver has strived to create a beer list that includes a little bit of everything, from Belgian Blondes, to IPAs of many kinds, to stouts, a Belgian trippel, and some barrel-aged beers. Given the variety, visitors of all ilks will likely find something at Rough Draft that suits.

SAINT ARCHER BREWING COMPANY (Miramar)

saintarcher
brewery.com

9550 Distribution Ave.
San Diego CA 92121

(858) 225-2337

Every day: 3 pm–9 pm

2

WHEN SAINT ARCHER FIRST opened its tasting room doors in May 2013, it had been one of San Diego's most highly anticipated debuts. Savvy marketing, cool design, and a well-crafted "surfer-X Games" image made the brand appealing from the get-go (especially to the 20-something crowd).

As a brand-new brewery, Saint Archer hit the ground running—and in a big way. Their 17,000-square-foot brewery space and 30-barrel system make for a large initial footprint and offer plenty of room for a long bar and an expansive tasting area.

tasting room	yes
beers on tap	4+
cask / nitro	yes
tours	yes
kegs	no
growlers	32 & 64 oz.
bottles	12 & 22 oz.
six packs	yes
merchandise	yes
kid friendly	yes
dog friendly	no
seating	good
food	food trucks & nearby

BEER	COLOR	AROMA	TASTE
blonde 4.8% (kolsch)	golden yellow	light, bready malt	light crisp malt with notes of biscuits; crisp and clean
pale ale 5.2%	golden yellow orange	honey, caramel, with citrus and floral notes	lemon and honey balanced by crisp hoppy bitterness
IPA 6.8%	deep golden honey	floral and honey hops	citrus, lemon, grapefruit; crisp and clean with medium mouthfeel and bitter finish

• tasters, pints, and flights available

SAINT ARCHER also hit the ground with two talented and experienced brewers—Ray Astamendi and Kim Lutz—both of whom have impressive pedigrees, and both previously from Maui Brewing. For a big brewery with big plans, the initial beer lineup is decidedly small and focused, the core being three very drinkable ales, the highest of which is below 7% ABV.

SAN DIEGO BREWING COMPANY (Grantville)

sandiegobrewing.com

2

10450 Friars Rd.
San Diego, CA 92120
(619) 284-2739
Mon–Thur: 11 am–12 am
Fri: 11 am–1 pm
Sat: 9 am–1 pm
Sun: 9 am–11 pm

SAN DIEGO BREWING MAY BE ONE of the unsung heroes in San Diego's craft beer narrative. According to co-founder Lee Doxalter, Callahan's (which became SD Brewing) was the first brewpub and then multi-tap brewery in the county (post-Prohibition). Soon after Karl Strauss opened the city's first craft brewery in 1989, Doxalter and co-founder Scott Stamp opened Callahan's, which quickly started brewing and offering a then-unheard-of 12-tap selection of handcrafted beers.

Today, San Diego Brewing is housed inside a large brewpub that offers a full menu and a choice of tables, booths,

tasting room	bar / restaurant
beers on tap	45 / 8 house
cask / nitro	yes
tours	no
kegs	no
growlers	64 oz.
bottles	no
six packs	no
merchandise	yes
kid friendly	yes
dog friendly	no
seating	very good
food	full menu

BEER	COLOR	AROMA	TASTE
grantville gold 4.5% (pale ale)	medium golden straw	light malt and hint of hops	light, crisp maltiness balanced by clean, slightly sweet finish
infinitude IPA 7%	medium golden orange	hoppy citrus, pine, lemon, and honey	lemon, honey, pine, grapefruit, tropical fruit with medium mouthfeel; finishes with a touch of sweet before final bitterness
old town nut brown 5.7%	medium reddish brown	caramel malt with toffee, chocolate, and coffee	caramel, coffee, chocolate with a medium mouthfeel and slightly sweet finish
old saxon old ale 8%	dark cherry brown	caramel, toffee, dried fruit, bread	vanilla, caramel, malty with winey, bourbon notes; rich mouthfeel
callahan's blueberry wheat 4.5%	light golden yellow	blueberry	blueberry flavors with crisp, light, and slightly sweet malty finish

• tasters, half pints, pints, 25 oz. mugs, and flights available

or seats at the spacious bar. The atmosphere is family-friendly and informal, so don't come looking for a hipster "happening scene."

BREWMASTER JEFF DRUM'S BEER LINEUP is intentionally straightforward and accessible, so drinkers of all tastes and palates will find something that suits. He does well-crafted, mostly American-style beers that are easy to drink and go well with food. (IPA lovers will be especially happy with the delicious Infinitude IPA.)

SAN MARCOS BREWERY & GRILL (San Marcos)

sanmarcosbrewery.com 1

(760) 471-0050

Mon: 11 am–9:30 pm
Tue: 11 am–10 pm
Wed, Thur: 11 am–10:30 pm
Fri: 11 am–11:30 pm
Sat: 11 am–11:30 pm
Sun: 10:30 am–9:30 pm

SAN MARCOS BREWERY & GRILL has long been a fixture in the San Marcos brew scene. As a full restaurant that houses a micro brewery inside, it provides a comfortable atmosphere for craft beer fans and their families to have lunch or dinner in addition to tasting a nice selection of beers.

Tables, booths, and seating are available inside, and there is also an outdoor patio. Unlike many of the newest tasting rooms and brewpubs in the area, the vibe here is deliberately not "hip and trendy," but rather comfortable and quiet.

tasting room	bar / restaurant
beers on tap	8 house / 8 guest
cask / nitro	cask
tours	by request
kegs	2 & 5 gal.
growlers	64 oz.
bottles	22 oz.
six packs	no
merchandise	yes
kid friendly	yes
dog friendly	no
seating	very good
food	full menu

BEER	COLOR	AROMA	TASTE
honey ale 5.5%	dark golden	sweet honey	crisp, hoppy, light refreshing malt
hefeweizen 5.6%	hazy, golden yellow	banana, clove, bready yeastiness	tropical fruits, banana, clove, bubble gum
san marcos brewing IPA 8%	dark golden	sweet honey	sweet, mild maltiness and hop character
amber ale 6%	caramel	caramel maltiness	sweet malt, caramel, nuts
Belgian gold 8%	light straw yellow	tropical fruits, bubble gum, bready yeast	light, crisp, fruity
Scottish ale 5.1%	medium caramel, big, frothy head	molasses, bread	sweet, malty, nutty, light bodied
oatmeal stout 6%	deep, dark reddish brown, rich frothy head	roasted coffee, chocolate	malty chocolate, vanilla, coffee, light, clean mouthfeel

• tasters, pints, and flights available

THE ROTATING LINEUP OF 8 solid house-brewed beers is augmented by 8 additional guest taps that provide a selection from some of San Diego's top breweries.

SOCIETE BREWING CO. (Kearny Mesa)

societebrewing.com

2

8262 Clairemont Mesa Blvd.
San Diego, CA 92111
(858) 598-5409

Mon–Thur: 12 pm–9 pm
Fri, Sat: 12 pm–10 pm
Sun: 12 pm–6 pm

WHEN SOCIETE FIRST OPENED their doors in May 2012, there were already plenty of great beers being made in San Diego. To the faint-of-heart brewer, it might have seemed as if the field was too crowded to even consider launching another San Diego brewery. But co-founders Doug Constantiner and Travis Smith were convinced that if they made truly great beer, the world would find a place for them. And it did. Big time.

Housed in a large industrial office park, the classy but rustic tasting room offers ample space for the many fans who now regularly flock to the brewery. There's some room to sip a

tasting room	yes
beers on tap	8+
cask / nitro	no
tours	saturday
kegs	no
growlers	64 oz.
bottles	no
six packs	no
merchandise	yes
kid friendly	yes
dog friendly	yes
seating	good
food	weekend food truck

BEER	COLOR	AROMA	TASTE
harlot 6% (Belgian extra pale)	light golden yellow	light hops balanced with bready Belgian yeast and tropical fruit esters	multi-layered tropical fruit, spice, light malt, and yeastiness; crisp and balanced
apprentice 7.5% (IPA)	medium golden yellow	citrus and piney hops	bright citrus and hints of lemon with full mouthfeel and pleasing bitterness
pupil 7.5% (IPA)	deep golden yellow	honey, grapefruit, and guava	tropical fruit, with hints of honey and grapefruit, finishes dry with smooth bitterness
widow 9% (Belgian dark ale)	deep copper	roasty malt, caramel, toffee, spicy Belgian yeast	caramel, toffee maltiness balanced by crisp hops and bready yeastiness; finishes mostly dry with a hint of sweetness
butcher 9.8% (imperial stout)	deep chocolate brown	roasty coffee, chocolate, toast, and vanilla	rich maltiness with bitter chocolate; rich mouthfeel and semi-dry finish

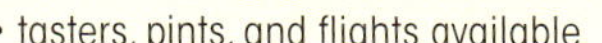

• tasters, pints, and flights available

pint outside as well, but the long, high communal tables inside provide for a much more social experience.

SOCIETE'S LINEUP IS BASED on a two-pronged approach that includes beers in the "San Diego style" and beers in the "Belgian style." The San Diego line tends toward richly flavored hoppy beers, while the Belgian side focuses primarily on Belgian-style ales that range from light and floral to dark and rich. All Societe's beers are outstanding, but hop-heads should not miss an opportunity to taste The Pupil IPA or any of its relatives: The Apprentice, The Dandy, and the award-winning Roustabout.

STONE BREWING CO. (Escondido)

stonebrewing.com

1999 Citracado Pkwy.
Escondido, CA 92029

(760) 294-7866

Sun–Thur: 11 am–11 pm
Fri, Sat: 11 am–12 am

1

IF YOU'VE HEARD OF SAN DIEGO craft beer, you've heard of Stone. As perhaps Southern California's greatest brewing success story (thus far), Stone has cultivated vast minions of loyal, dedicated, die-hard fans all over the world. Not surprisingly, the "cult of Stone" is often compared to that of a rock band.

Stone's main facility in Escondido is big, and getting bigger. The concrete building that houses the enormous brewery space and administrative offices fell short in terms of capacity awhile back. The brewery shares the building with the company's restaurant, Stone World

tasting room	bar / bistro
beers on tap	9 house / 22+ guest
cask / nitro	cask
tours	every day
kegs	5 & 15.5 gal.
growlers	40 & 67 oz.
bottles	22 oz. & 500 ml.
six packs	yes
merchandise	yes
kid friendly	yes
dog friendly	no
seating	very good
food	full menu

BEER	COLOR	AROMA	TASTE	
stone pale ale 5.4%	deep copper orange	citrus, pine, caramel malts	malt forward with hoppy notes of citrus and pine and a bitter finish	●●
stone smoked porter 5.9%	deep copper brown	smoky with chocolate and roasted malt	chocolate with great smoky balance; crisp but with medium mouthfeel; finishes bitter	●●
stone IPA 6.9%	deep golden yellow	citrus, pine, grapefruit, honey	honey, lemon, grapefruit, pine; crisp with medium mouthfeel and bitter finish	●●
arrogant bastard ale 7.2%	dark copper amber	caramel malt up front; citrus hops	big malty caramel followed by citrus hop crispness; rich mouthfeel with bitter finish	●●
stone ruination IPA 7.7%	medium golden yellow	big citrus hops, tropical fruit, lemon, grass	crisp citrus and honey with pine notes and medium mouthfeel	●●
stone sublimely self-righteous ale 8.7%	rich caramel brown	big lemon, grapefruit, and tropical fruit	lemon, orange, grapefruit with rich solid malt backbone and bitter finish	●●

• tasters, half pints, pints, and flights available

Bistro & Gardens, which offers beautiful indoor and outdoor settings replete with ponds, waterfalls, fire pits, and lots of greenery.

SUPER-TALENTED HEAD BREWER MITCH STEELE oversees the production of too many great beers to summarize here. If you're anything of a hop-head, you'll love the variety of aggressively hopped full-flavored options on tap. If you prefer other styles, such as barleywines, stouts, porters, or Belgians (which are plenty hoppy!), there's always an array of excellent selections from which to choose. No matter what you try, you won't go wrong.

Other Tasting Locations:
South Park; Oceanside; Pasadena

STONE BREWING CO. (Liberty Station)

stonebrewing.com 3

2816 Historic Decatur Rd.
#116, San Diego, CA 92106

(760) 294-7899

Sun–Thur: 10 am–11 pm
Fri, Sat: 10 am–12 am

STONE FANS IN THE MORE SOUTHERN neighborhoods of San Diego had reason to rejoice in May 2013, when Stone Brewing World Bistro & Gardens—Liberty Station opened its doors. The huge new space delivers everything the hard-core Stone groupie craves and more, including plenty of rock and water features, bocce courts, and an outdoor movie-viewing lawn.

A good deal of the original historic military barracks structure has been incorporated into the renovation, which covers about 55,000 square feet and includes private rooms for

tasting room	bar / bistro
beers on tap	10 house / 30+ guest
cask / nitro	cask
tours	by request
kegs	5 & 15.5 gal.
growlers	40 & 67 oz.
bottles	22 oz. & 500 ml.
six packs	yes
merchandise	yes
kid friendly	yes
dog friendly	outside patio
seating	very good
food	full menu

BEER	COLOR	AROMA	TASTE
witty moron 4.9% (black wit)	dark brown with amber tinge	chocolate, nuts, yeasty esters	crisp maltiness with nutty, bready notes; nice yeastiness with crisp finish
stone 12/15 IPA 5.5%	golden orange	big citrus with honeysuckle and grapefruit notes	big citrus and floral hoppiness with a clean, crisp, bitter finish
angry & wit 6.9% (wheat IPA)	golden orange	yeasty esters with hints of mint and eucalyptus	bready and hoppy with slight notes of eucalyptus and a bitter finish

• tasters, half pints, pints, and flights available

meetings and special events, as well as expansive indoor and outdoor seating areas.

PERHAPS THE BEST ASPECT of the new location is that it offers brewer Kris Ketcham and his team a chance to explore beer styles and recipes that are not feasible on a larger scale. Though this location offers the entire Stone lineup, it also offers small-batch specialty brews created on site with a 20-barrel system. Given the small production of these beers, they change daily, so no beer is guaranteed to reappear on any kind of schedule (some great wit beers were on tap for our visit). Luckily, no matter what's pouring, you can bet it'll be excellent.

STUMBLEFOOT BREWING COMPANY (San Marcos)

stumblefoot.com

1784 La Costa Meadows Dr.
#103, San Marcos, CA 92078
(760) 522-9624
Mon–Wed: Closed
Thur: 4 pm–7 pm
Fri: 3 pm–8 pm
Sat: 12 pm–6 pm
Sun: 1 pm–5 pm

LONGTIME HOMEBREWERS (and brothers) Bill Randolph and Pat Horton took the leap in March of 2012, when they turned their amateur brewing skills professional and opened Stumblefoot. Though they went from brewing 5-gallon batches to brewing on a 5-barrel system, the brewery still has the cozy feeling of a garage operation.

Housed—as so many San Diego breweries are—in a small, nondescript industrial park, the Stumblefoot tasting room feels a bit dark and cramped, but the friendly speakeasy-type atmosphere more than makes up for the lack of space.

tasting room	yes
beers on tap	12+
cask / nitro	no
tours	no
kegs	5 & 15.5 gal.
growlers	64 oz.
bottles	no
six packs	no
merchandise	yes
kid friendly	yes
dog friendly	yes
seating	no
food	no

BEER	COLOR	AROMA	TASTE
schwarzbier 5%	dark brown	malty, roasty, slight hop notes	malty, chocolate, coffee with light mouthfeel and slightly sweet finish
vixen dunkelweizen 6%	dark copper brown	bready, wheaty esters, hints of bubble gum and tropical fruit	bread and fruit yeastiness balanced with malt and crisp finish
back to black IPA 6.75%	deep brown	citrus and piney hops	citrus, orange, grapefruit with a firm malt backbone and medium mouthfeel
flakey robin Belgian sour 7.5%	medium orange copper	tropical fruit, citrus, Belgian yeastiness	citrus, tropical fruit, warm bready yeast, crisp, tart, and full flavored

• tasters, half pints, pints, and flights available

THE LINEUP AT STUMBLEFOOT is governed by what Bill and Pat feel like making (translation: what they feel like drinking) at any given time. They have based many of their offerings on German-inspired beer styles that they enjoy best, and regularly do some of the less-represented styles, such as Dunkelweizen and Schwarzbier, particularly well.

THE BEER COMPANY (Downtown)

thebeerco.net

3

602 W. 6th Ave.
San Diego, CA
92101

(619) 398-0707

Every day: 11 am–2 am

FOR BEER BREWED ON THE PREMISES and served along with a full bar-pub style menu, The Beer Company is one of the three top choices downtown.

A spacious restaurant surrounds a very large bar, which offers a wide selection of both Beer Co. brews as well as excellent guest beers. Though it is perfectly family-friendly, the large, loud flat screens and the imposing bar make the space feel more like a bar than a brewpub.

tasting room	bar / restaurant
beers on tap	28
cask / nitro	cask
tours	no
kegs	no
growlers	64 oz.
bottles	no
six packs	no
merchandise	yes
kid friendly	yes
dog friendly	no
seating	very good
food	full menu

BEER	COLOR	AROMA	TASTE
barn owl saison 6.5%	medium golden yellow-orange	bready esters, orange peel, clove	clove, orange peel, allspice, medium mouthfeel with malty, crisp finish
wyatt earp red 7%	medium reddish orange	light malt	nutty, toast, light malt, light mouthfeel with bitter finish
chin checker dark (rye) IPA 7%	medium orange brown	pine, citrus hops, bready toasted malt	pine, citrus, honey with malt chocolate notes and a pleasing bitter finish
level 5 barleywine 10%	hazy, deep orange brown	raisin, dry fruit, hints of bourbon	dry fruit, molasses, vanilla, with bourbon notes, crisp but rich mouthfeel with medium sweet finish

• tasters, pints, and flights available

AN AVERAGE OF EIGHT or so Beer Co. beers make up the core lineup, which encompasses a variety of classic styles. Overall, the beers are well balanced—they go well with food, are aimed to please a wide variety of beer drinkers, and they deliver flavor.

THORN ST. BREWERY (North Park)

thornstreetbrew.com
3176 Thorn St.
San Diego, CA 92104
(619) 501-2739
Mon, Tue: Closed
Wed, Thur: 4 pm–9 pm
Fri: 4 pm–10 pm
Sat: 2 pm–10 pm
Sun: 2 pm–8 pm

3

ON A SEEMINGLY QUIET CORNER of a seemingly quiet, residential street in North Park sits Thorn St. Brewery. Opened (in a soft way) at the end of 2012, this small operation fits right into its surroundings and feels as if it truly belongs in the neighborhood.

The tasting room facilities at Thorn St. are actually two separate—and very different—spaces. From the street, you enter a cozy, low-ceilinged room covered in dark wood and lighted with sleek, modern fixtures. Walk through that space to the back room and you'll find a large, nicely designed,

tasting room	yes
beers on tap	16
cask / nitro	nitro
tours	no
kegs	no
growlers	64 oz.
bottles	no
six packs	no
merchandise	yes
kid friendly	yes
dog friendly	yes
seating	good
food	nearby

BEER	COLOR	AROMA	TASTE
red IPA 6.8%	reddish caramel	pine and floral hops	hoppy, with a light malt, finishes bitter
cascadian IPA 6.9%	dark brownish red	floral hops, malt, hints of chocolate	light hop character balanced with light malt flavors
coffee stout 5.5%	deep, dark brown	light hints of roasted coffee and chocolate	vanilla, chocolate, macadamia nut, with up-front sweetness and dry finish
bohemian pilsner 5.6%	light golden yellow	light hints of malt and German hops	light maltiness, crisp, finishes clean and bitter
Belgian strong 8.3%	hazy golden	warm bread yeast, spice, and clove	clover honey, clove, hints of coriander

• tasters, pints, and flights available

multifaceted space with another bar, bar tables, sofas, and various other seating and standing options.

MOST OF THE THORN ST. LINEUP seems to focus on malt-forward beers inspired by North American and British styles along with some Belgian-style offerings. For a young brewery, they are producing an admirable number of beers, so there is a nice variety of brews for visitors to choose from.

WET 'N RECKLESS BREWING COMPANY (Mira Mesa)

wetnreckless.com

2

10054 Mesa Ridge Ct.
#132, San Diego, CA 92121
(858) 480-9381

Sun–Wed: Closed
Thur, Fri: 3:30 pm–10 pm
Sat: 2 pm–10 pm

SOMEWHAT HIDDEN AWAY in a typical office-park complex, Wet 'N Reckless is one of San Diego's smallest operating pro breweries. A nondescript garage-style brewery and tasting space houses a small and very basic operation that feels especially handmade.

There is virtually no seating to speak of, and exceptionally small counter/bars provide only enough space for two or three people to stand comfortably.

tasting room	yes
beers on tap	11
cask / nitro	no
tours	no
kegs	no
growlers	16, 32 & 64 oz.
bottles	no
six packs	no
merchandise	no
kid friendly	yes
dog friendly	yes
seating	limited
food	no

BEER	COLOR	AROMA	TASTE
pop my cherry ale 4.8%	golden orange	bready esters, hints of tropical fruit	tart, citrus, cherry with hint of bready yeastines
golden boy IPA 8%	cloudy; light golden yellow	light honey; esters	flat; off flavors of petrol
heavens belge ale 8.6%	golden orange	bready, yeasty esters with hint of tropical fruit	yeasty, tropical fruits, bubble gum; some off flavors
honey badger don't care ale 10.5%	brown	wet wool	sweet and gummy with low bitterness
down and out stout 7%	dark brown	chocolate, roasted coffee	chocolate and coffee notes with light mouthfeel and sweet finish

• tasters and pints available

OWNER-BREWER Dave Hyndman does his brewing on a 1.6-barrel system, making a range of beers that include IPAs, stout, and some Belgian-inspired ales.

WHITE LABS TASTING ROOM (Miramar)

whitelabs.com

2

9495 Candida St.
San Diego, CA 92126

(858) 693-3441

Mon–Sat: 12 pm–8 pm
Sun: Closed

WHEN WHITE LABS OPENED its new facility with a tasting room in 2012, they added a whole new—and distinctive—option to the beer-touring experience. As one of the world's premier yeast suppliers, White Labs has the unique ability to showcase the central role that yeast plays in the brewing process.

In their elegant and contemporary tasting room, White Labs offers visitors a selection of flights, each of which highlights the effects of different yeasts fermenting the same wort. The differences are truly fascinating. If you're a budding homebrewer, or simply interested in learning more about the brewing process, this is a stop you'll want to make.

tasting room	yes
beers on tap	32
cask / nitro	cask
tours	fri & sat
kegs	no
growlers	32 oz.
bottles	no
six packs	no
merchandise	yes
kid friendly	yes
dog friendly	no
seating	good
food	nearby

BEER	COLOR	AROMA	TASTE
Leeuwenhoek saison 4.25%	light yellow	bready, yeasty esters	tropical fruit with light malt and crisp, slightly bitter finish
Buchner pale ale 5.5%	golden yellow	bready, malty	biscuit with hints of banana and citrus; crisp and light
Hanson IPA 6.5%	medium golden amber	honey with caramel malt	honey and slightly sweet with a bitter finish
Pasteur porter 6%	deep dark brown	chocolate, coffee, vanilla	milk chocolate, roasted coffee, light mouthfeel with a dry finish

• tasters, pints, and flights available

IN ADDITION TO THE FLIGHTS, the White Labs tasting room also offers a few select core beers of their own, brewed by Joe Kurowski. When you're done "experimenting," you can try a pint of White Labs beer, each of which is brewed with a mix of yeasts to create unique flavor profiles.

SECTOR 1

SECTOR 2

SECTOR 3

MAP OF SAN DIEGO BREWERIES

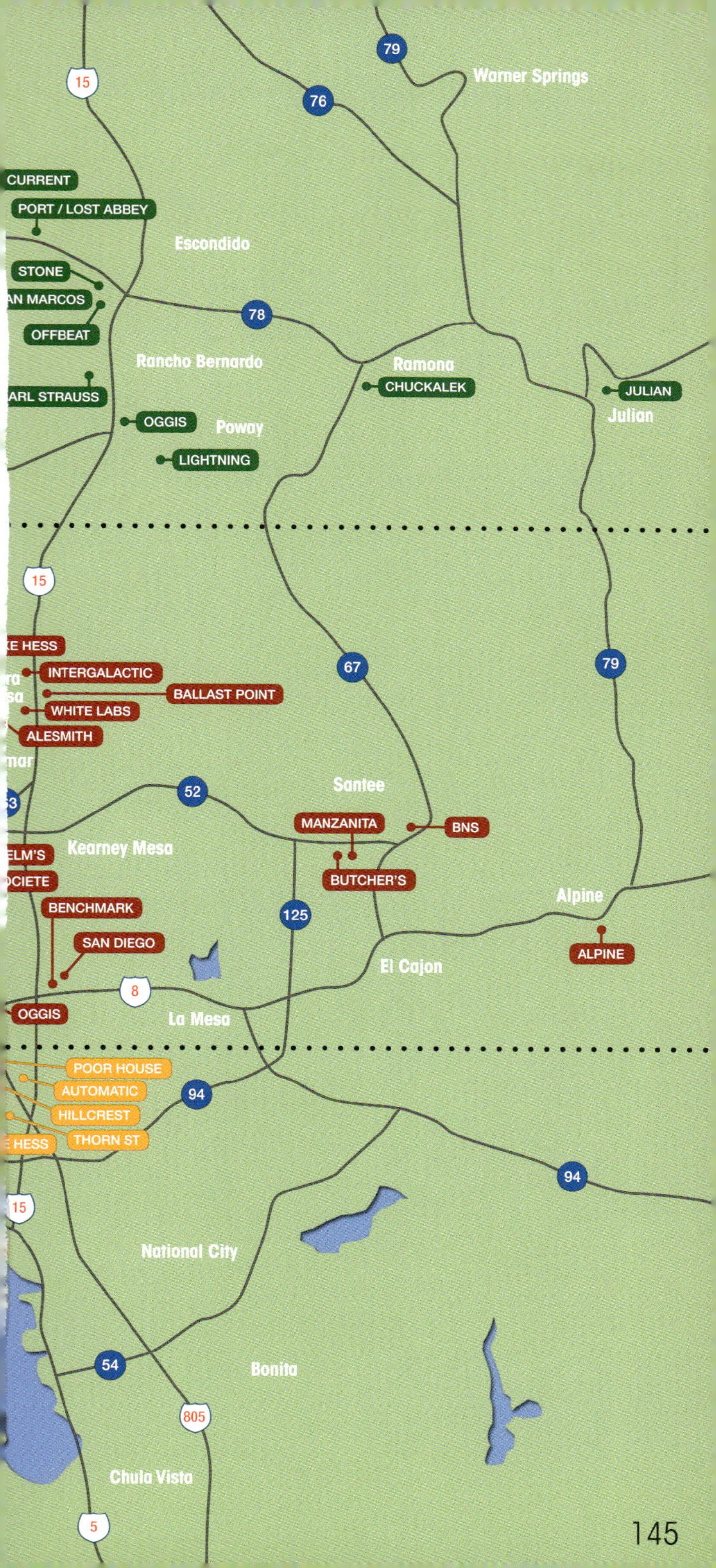

15
79
76
Warner Springs
CURRENT
PORT / LOST ABBEY
Escondido
STONE
78
OFFBEAT
Rancho Bernardo
Ramona
CHUCKALEK
JULIAN
Julian
OGGIS
Poway
LIGHTNING
15
67
79
INTERGALACTIC
BALLAST POINT
WHITE LABS
ALESMITH
52
Santee
MANZANITA
BNS
Kearney Mesa
BUTCHER'S
BENCHMARK
125
Alpine
SAN DIEGO
ALPINE
El Cajon
8
OGGIS
La Mesa
POOR HOUSE
AUTOMATIC
94
HILLCREST
THORN ST
94
15
National City
54
Bonita
805
Chula Vista
5

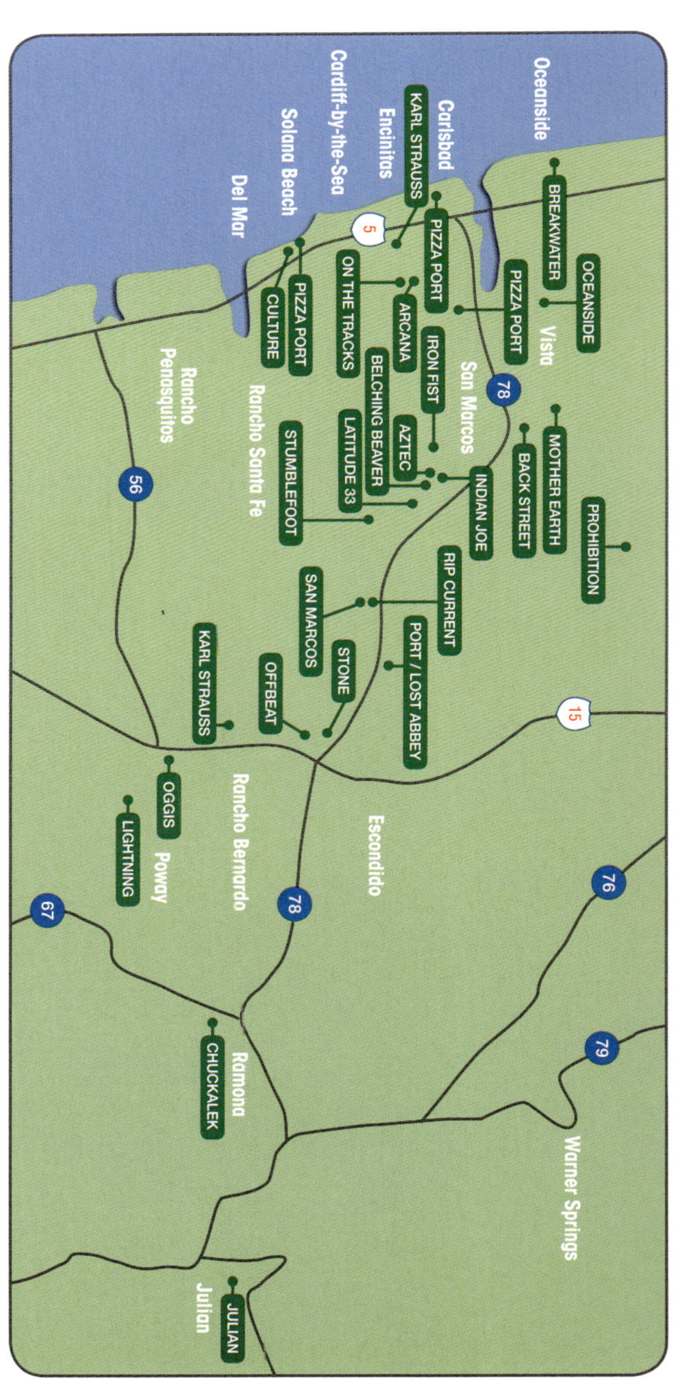

Oceanside
Carlsbad
Encinitas
Cardiff-by-the-Sea
Solana Beach
Del Mar
Vista
San Marcos
Rancho Santa Fe
Rancho Penasquitos
Rancho Bernardo
Escondido
Poway
Ramona
Warner Springs
Julian
BREAKWATER
OCEANSIDE
KARL STRAUSS
PIZZA PORT
PIZZA PORT
PIZZA PORT
CULTURE
ON THE TRACKS
ARCANA
IRON FIST
BELCHING BEAVER
AZTEC
LATITUDE 33
STUMBLEFOOT
INDIAN JOE
BACK STREET
MOTHER EARTH
PROHIBITION
RIP CURRENT
SAN MARCOS
PORT / LOST ABBEY
STONE
OFFBEAT
KARL STRAUSS
OGGIS
LIGHTNING
CHUCKALEK
JULIAN
5
78
56
15
78
67
76
79

SECTOR 2

HOME BREW MART / BP
PB ALE HOUSE
Pacific Beach
Mission Beach
La Jolla
KARL STRAUSS
ROCK BOTTOM
NEW ENGLISH
KARL STRAUSS
AMPLIFIED
5
KARL STRAUSS
KARL STRAUSS
CORONADO
Mission Valley
GORDON BIERSCH
ST. ARCHER
805
ROUGH DRAFT
Sorrento Valley
GREEN FLASH
WET 'N RECKLESS
Mira Mesa
Miramar
MIKE HESS
SOCIETE
HELM'S
163
OGGIS
ALESMITH
WHITE LABS
INTERGALACTIC
15
BENCHMARK
SAN DIEGO
Kearney Mesa
8
BALLAST POINT
La Mesa
52
125
MANZANITA
BUTCHER'S
Santee
67
El Cajon
BNS
Alpine
ALPINE
79

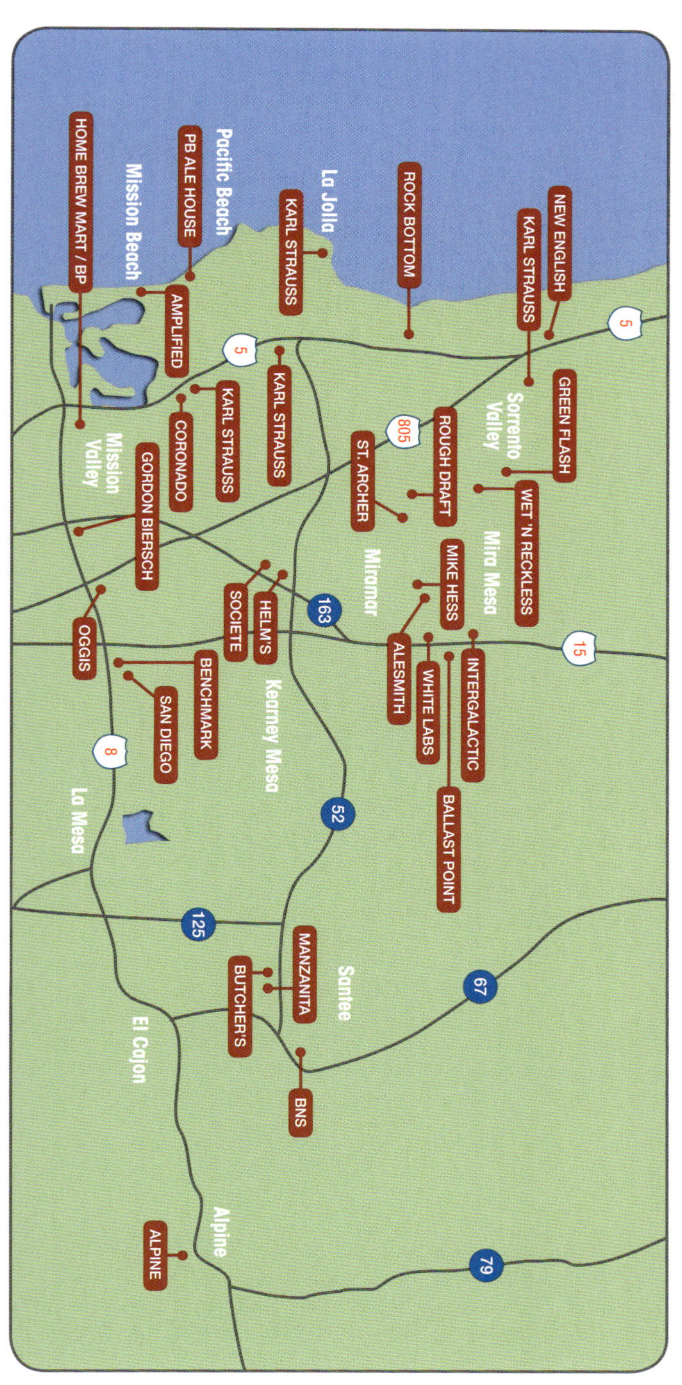

SECTOR 3

Point Loma
Ocean Beach
PIZZA PORT
MODERN TIMES
STONE
CORONADO
Coronado
ROCK BOTTOM
Downtown
KARL STRAUSS
MISSION
BEER CO
163
MIKE HESS
MONKEY PAW
15
THORN ST
HILLCREST
AUTOMATIC
POOR HOUSE
8
La Mesa
5
54
Chula Vista
805
National City
94
Bonita
94

HOP HEADS SECTOR 1

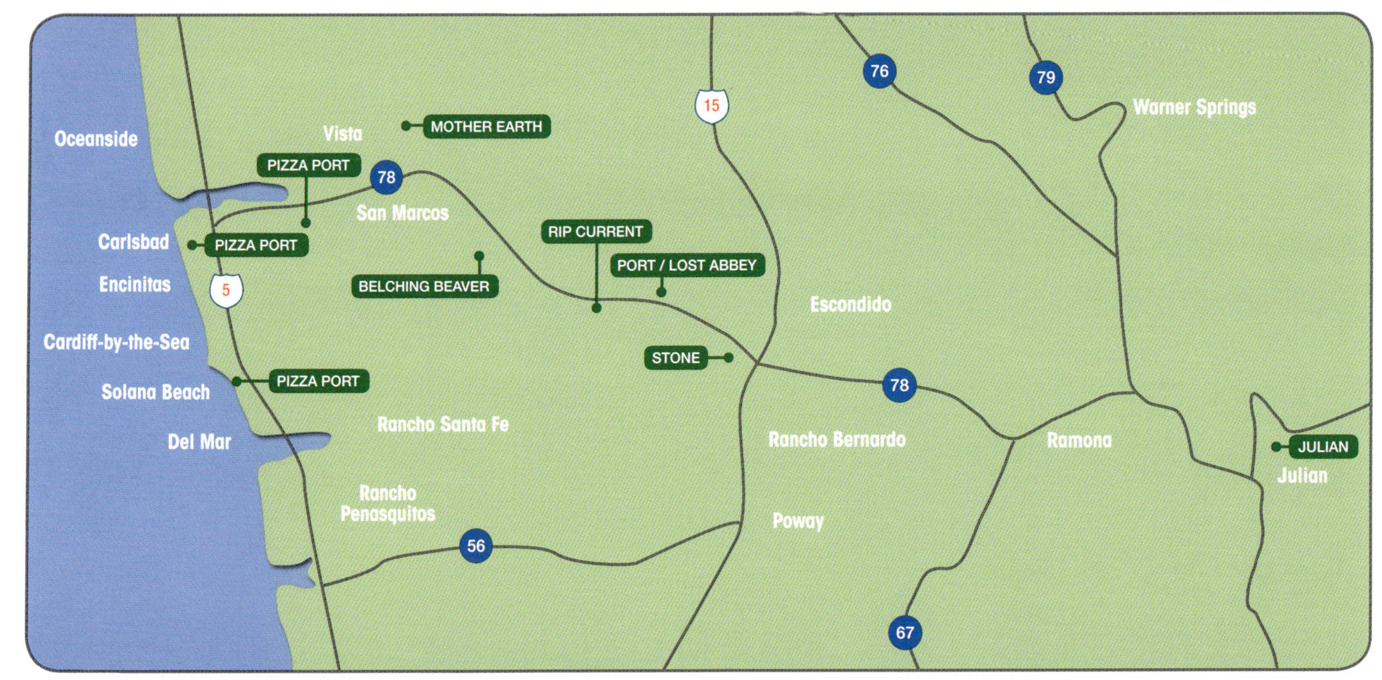

HOP HEADS SECTOR 2

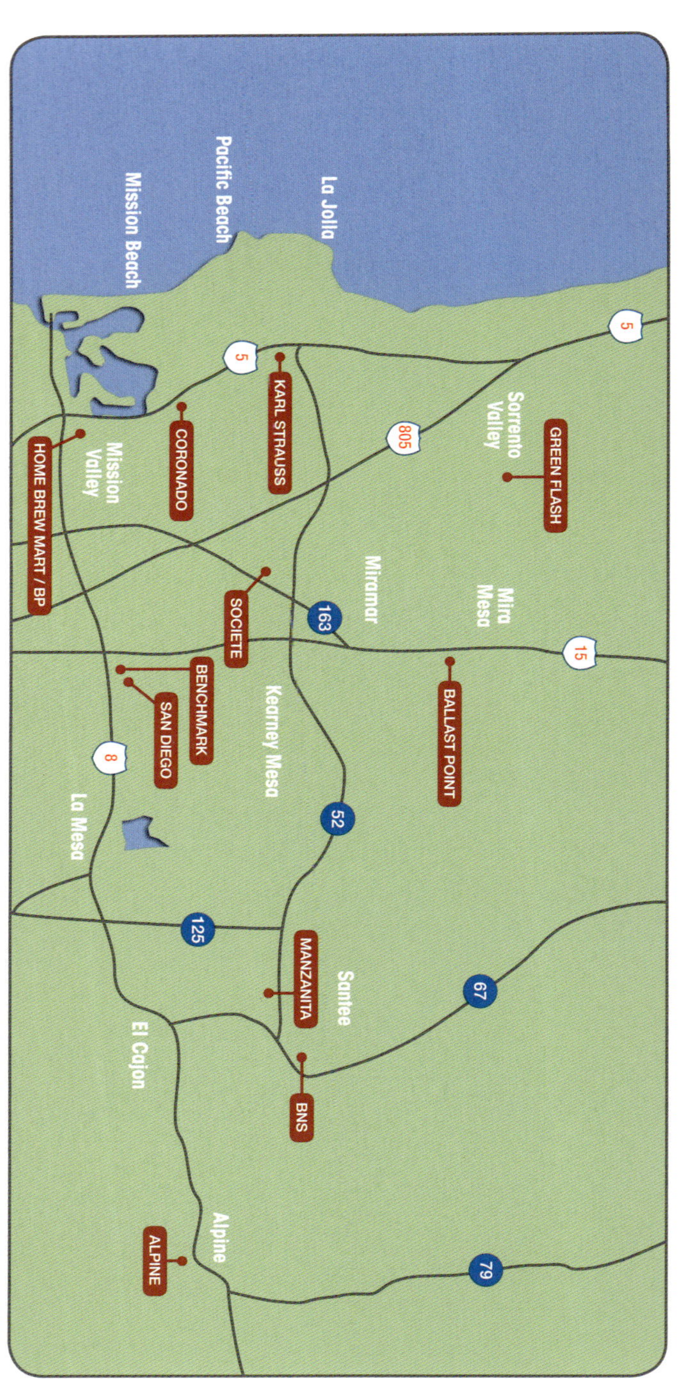

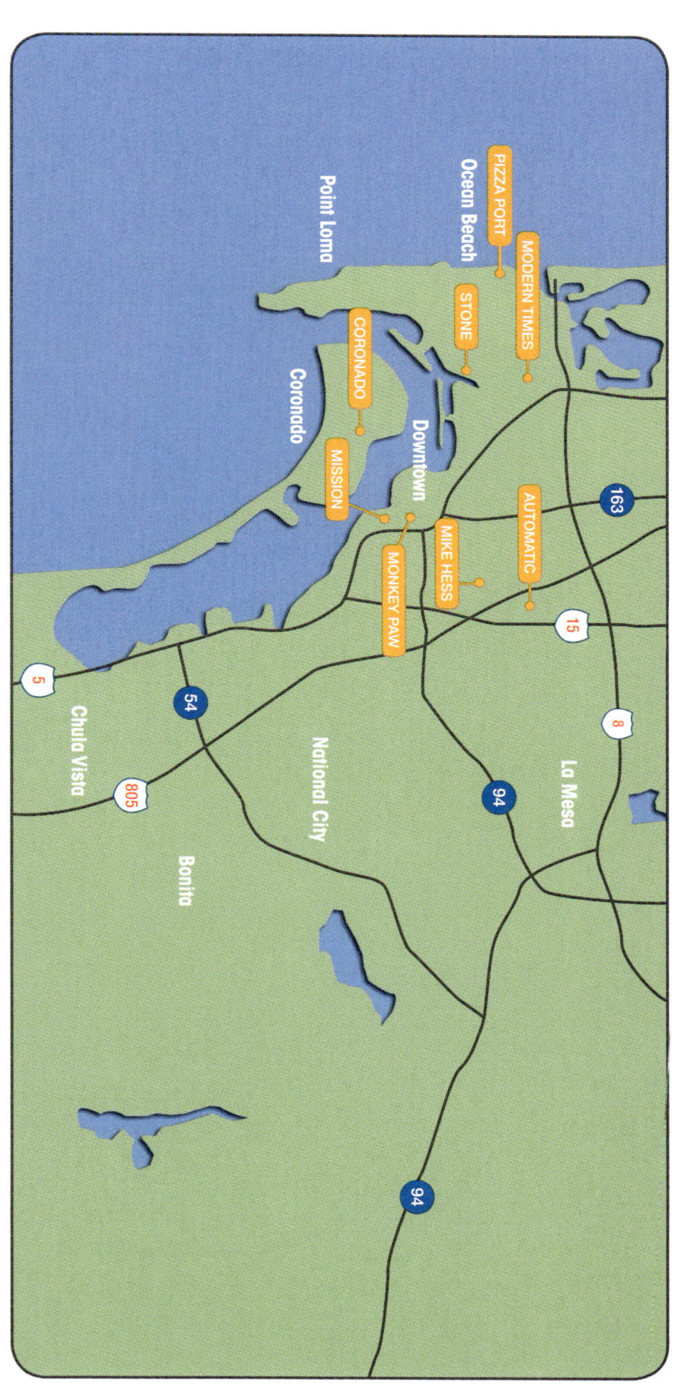
Point Loma
Ocean Beach
PIZZA PORT
MODERN TIMES
STONE
CORONADO
Coronado
Downtown
MISSION
AUTOMATIC
MIKE HESS
MONKEY PAW
163
15
5
54
8
805
94
Chula Vista
National City
La Mesa
Bonito
94

MALT MANIACS SECTOR 1

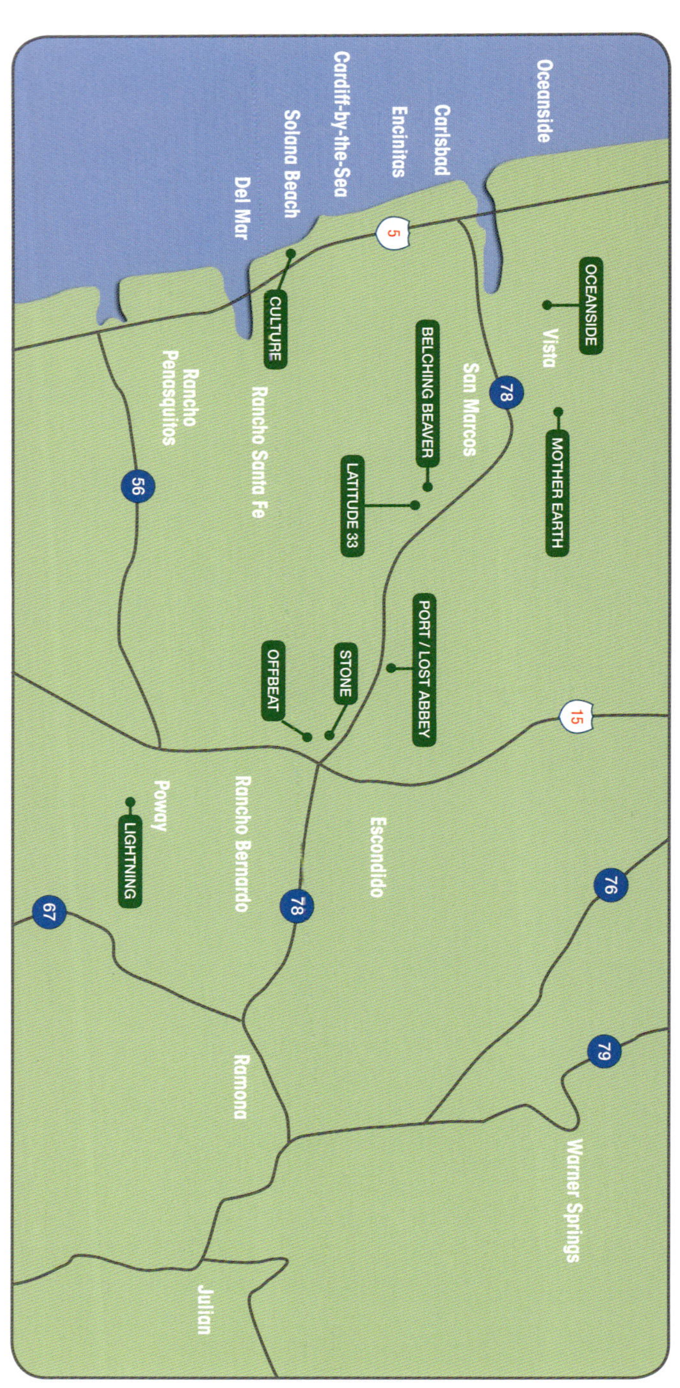

MALT MANIACS SECTOR 2

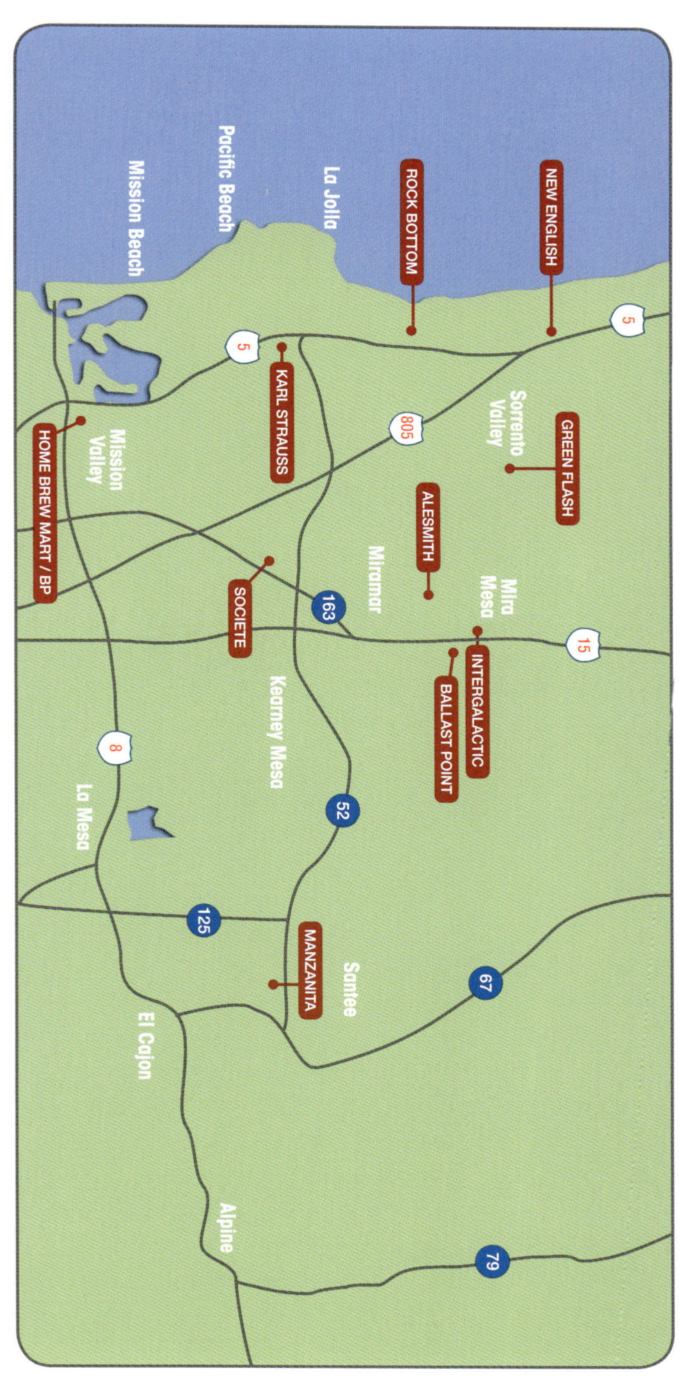

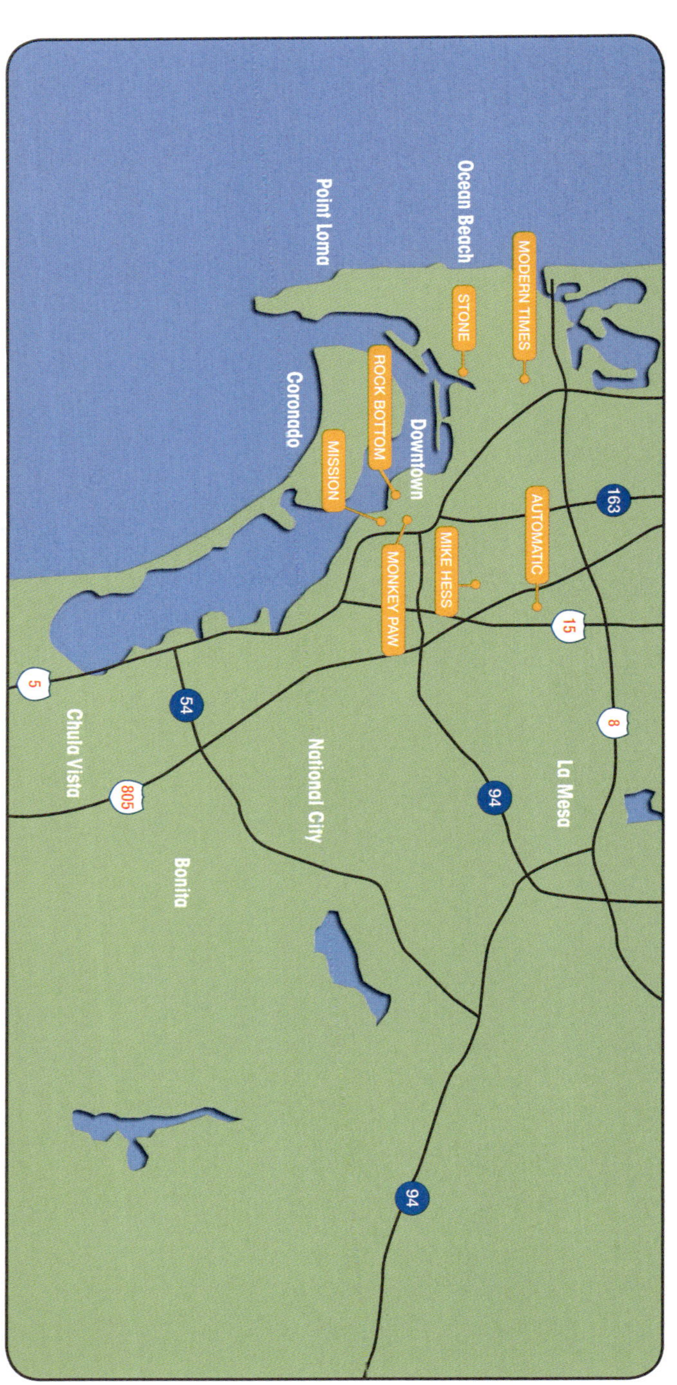
Point Loma
Ocean Beach
MODERN TIMES
STONE
ROCK BOTTOM
Coronado
Downtown
MISSION
AUTOMATIC
163
MIKE HESS
MONKEY PAW
15
5
54
8
Chula Vista
805
National City
94
La Mesa
Bonita
94

BELGIAN BELIEVERS SECTOR 1

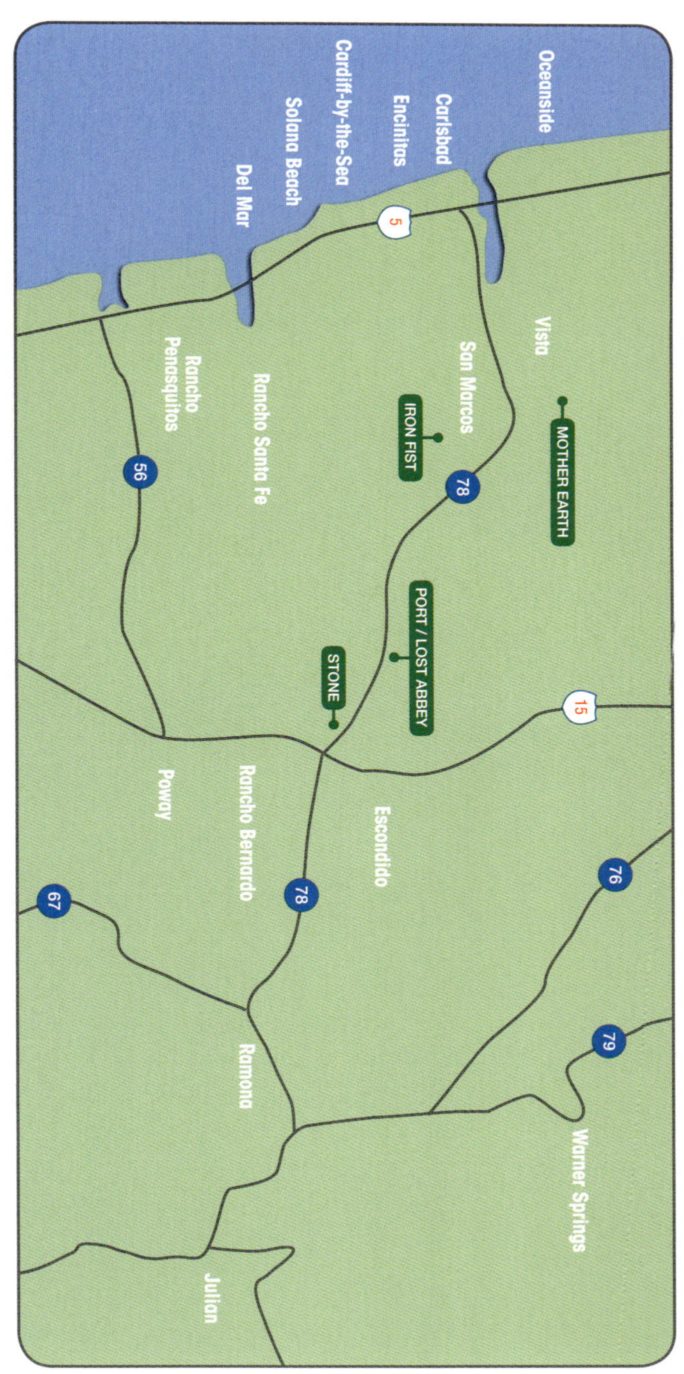

BELGIAN BELIEVERS SECTOR 2

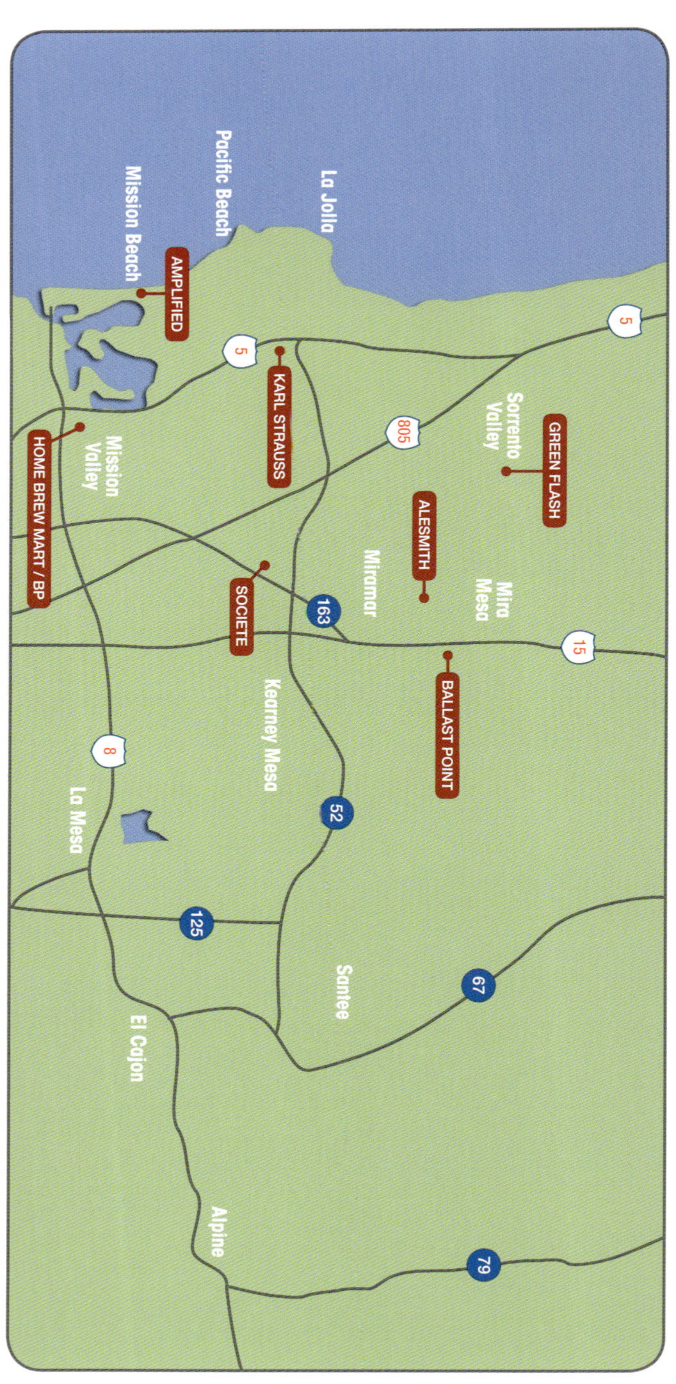

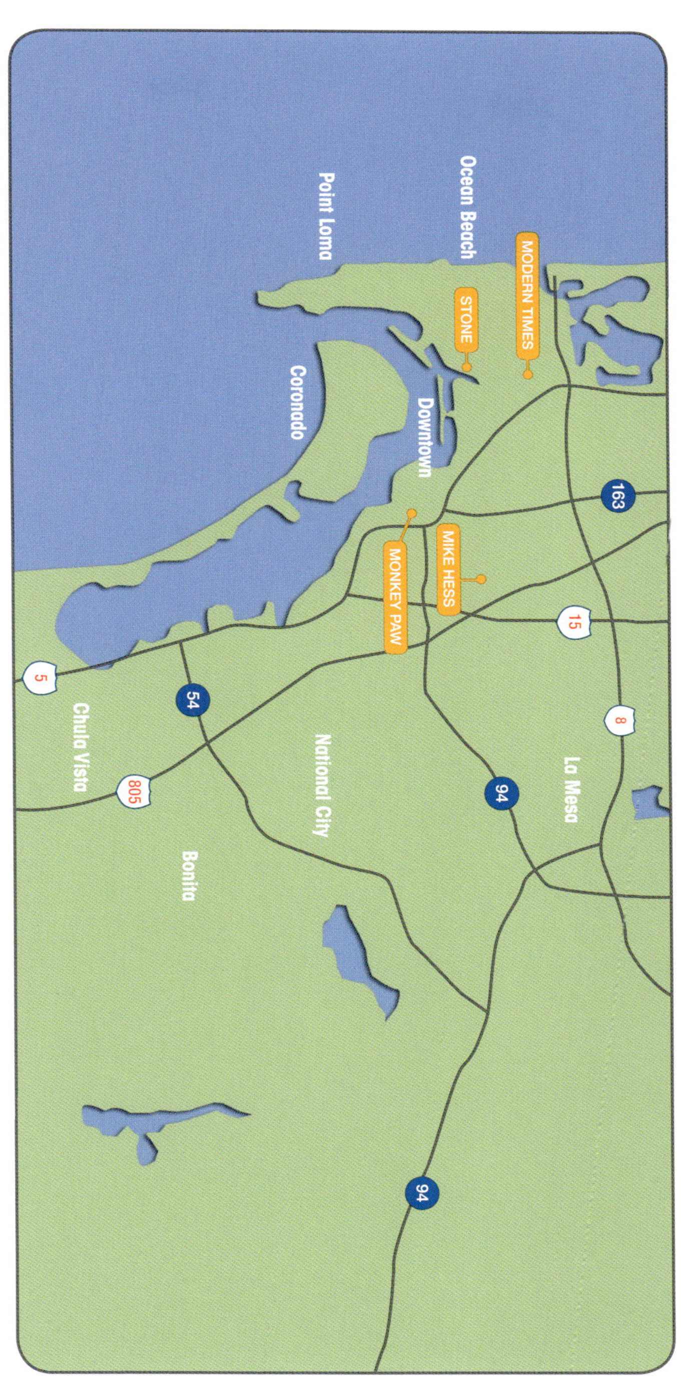
Ocean Beach
Point Loma
MODERN TIMES
STONE
Coronado
Downtown
163
MIKE HESS
MONKEY PAW
15
5
54
8
Chula Vista
National City
La Mesa
94
805
Bonita
94

HEF HOUNDS SECTOR 1

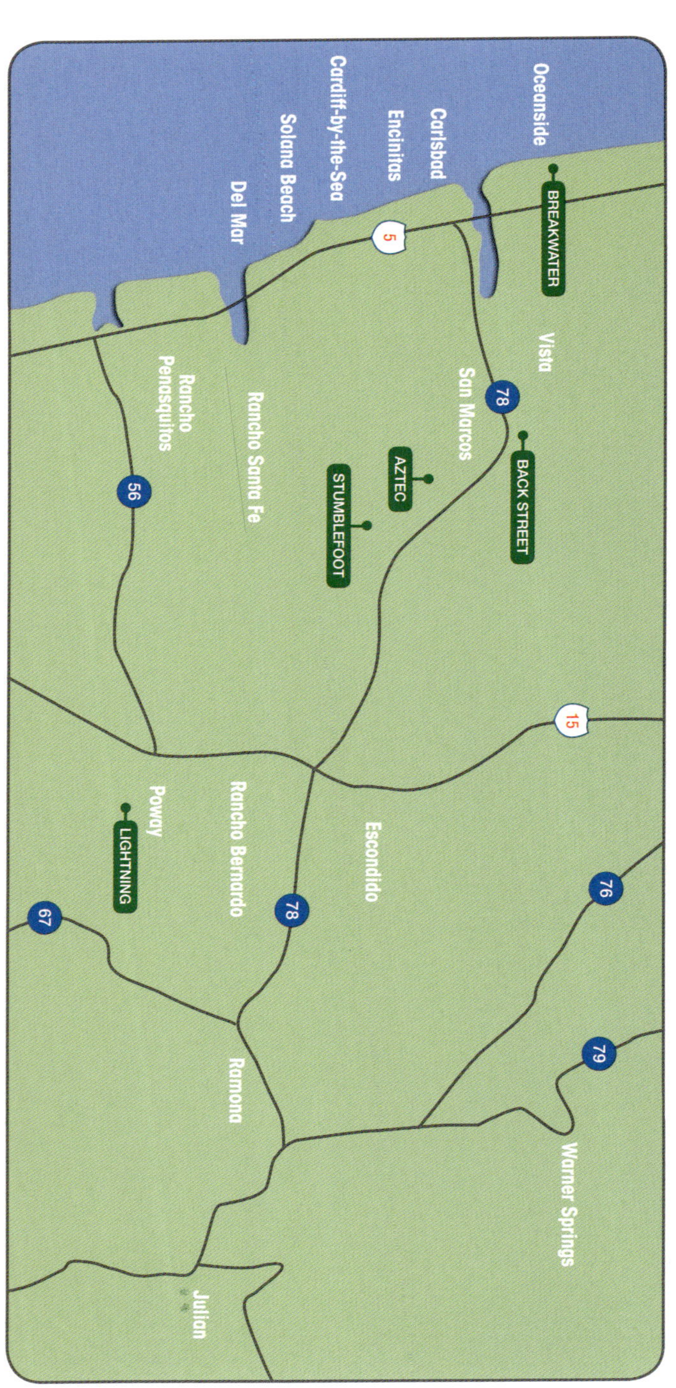

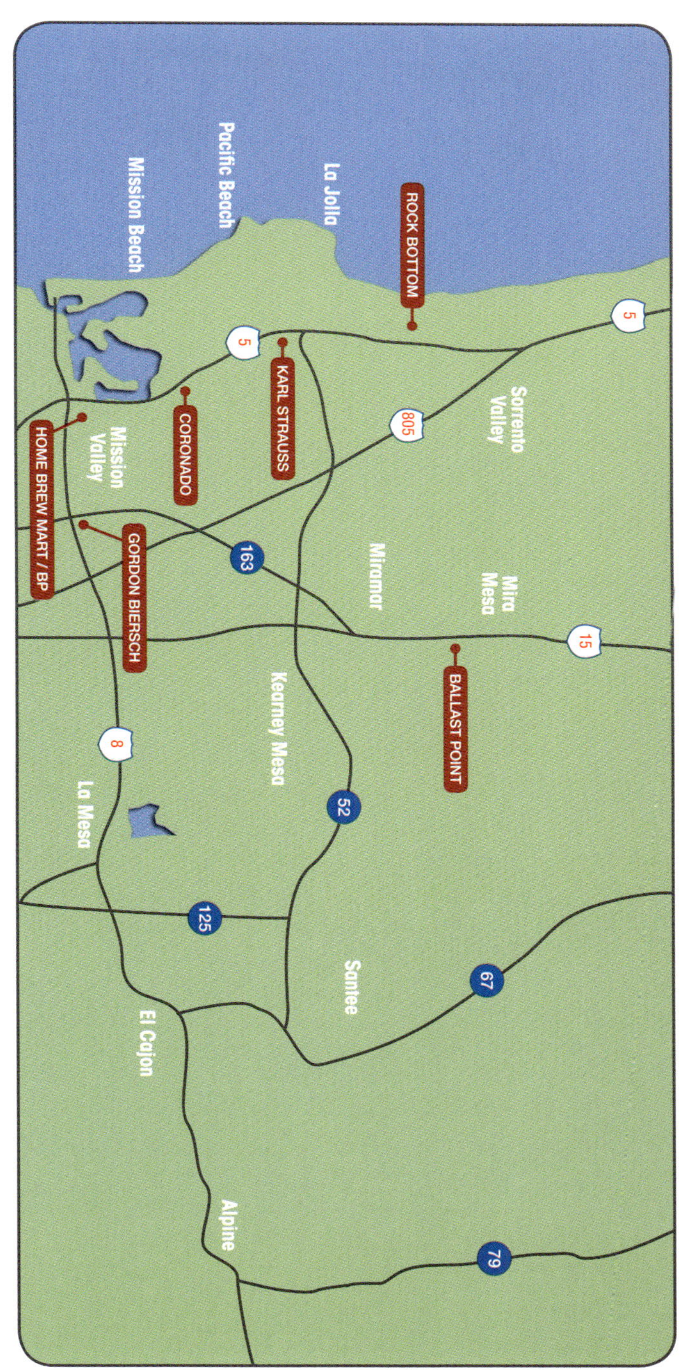
Mission Beach
Pacific Beach
La Jolla
ROCK BOTTOM
5
5
KARL STRAUSS
CORONADO
HOME BREW MART / BP
Mission Valley
805
Sorrento Valley
163
Miramar
Mira Mesa
GORDON BIERSCH
15
BALLAST POINT
Kearney Mesa
8
La Mesa
52
125
Santee
67
El Cajon
Alpine
79

HEF HOUNDS SECTOR 3

LAGER LOVERS SECTOR 1

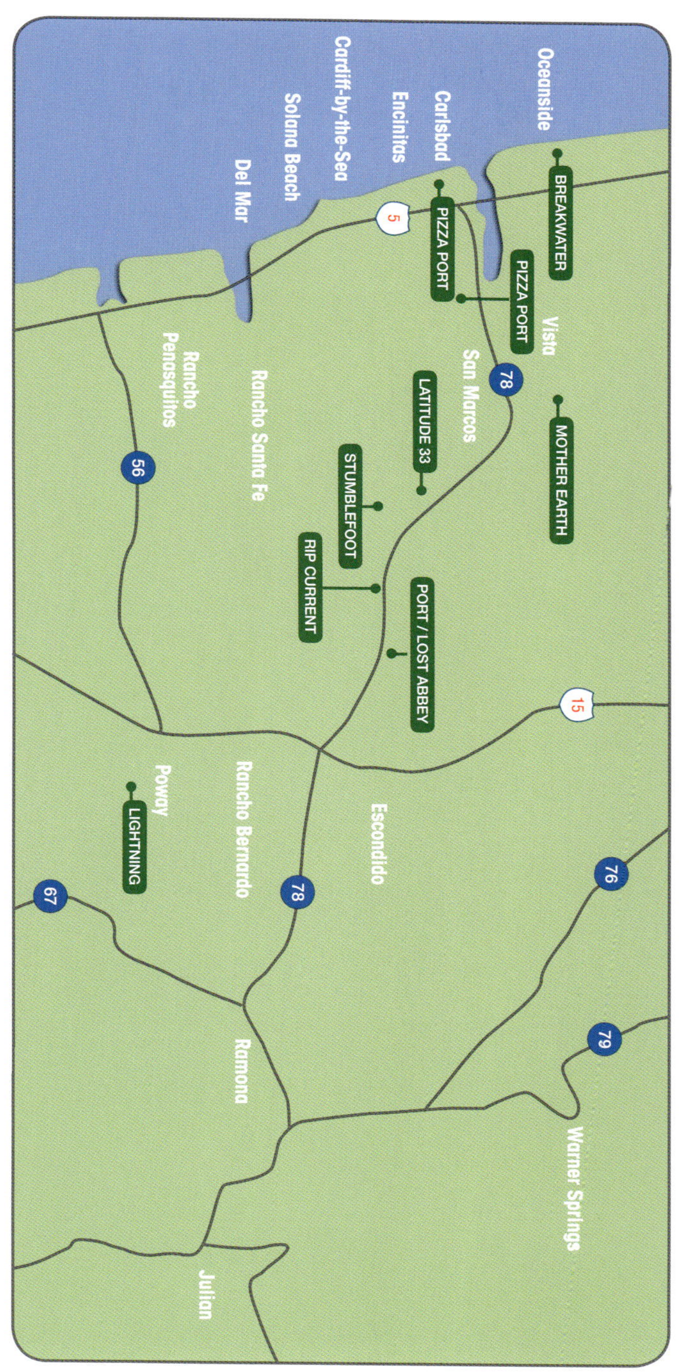

LAGER LOVERS SECTOR 2

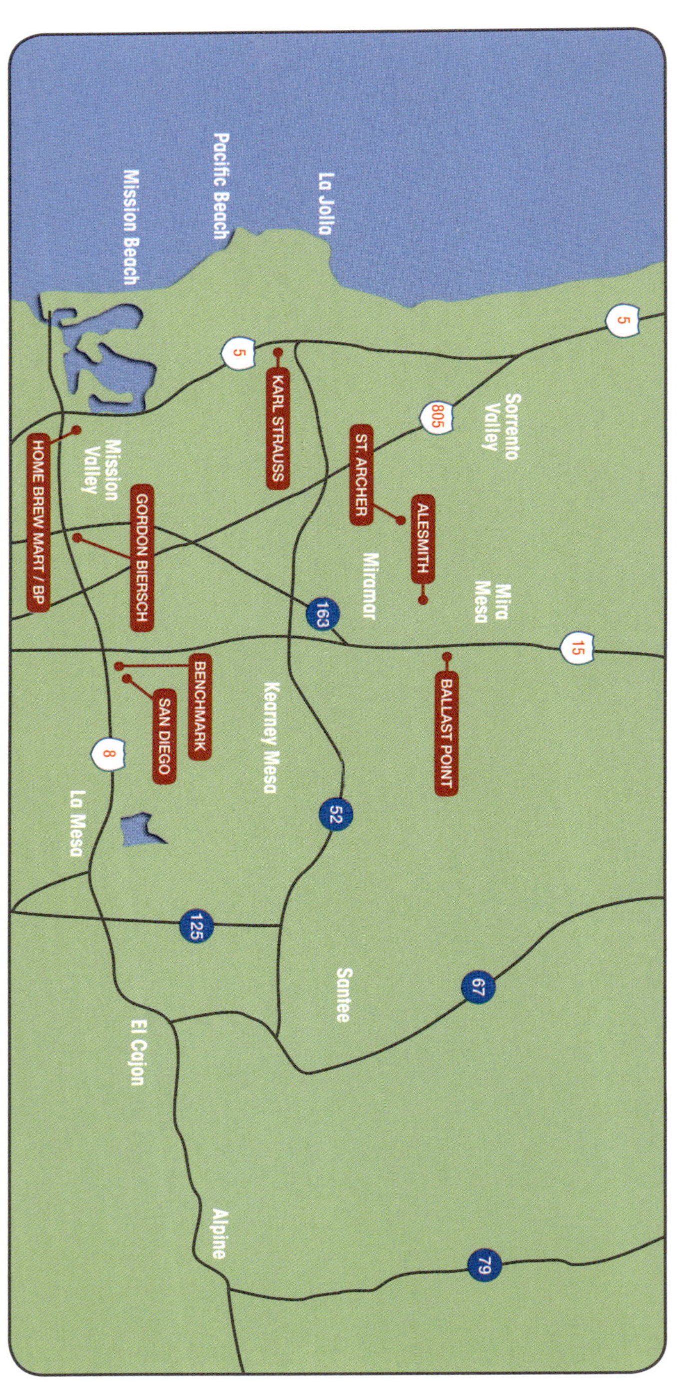

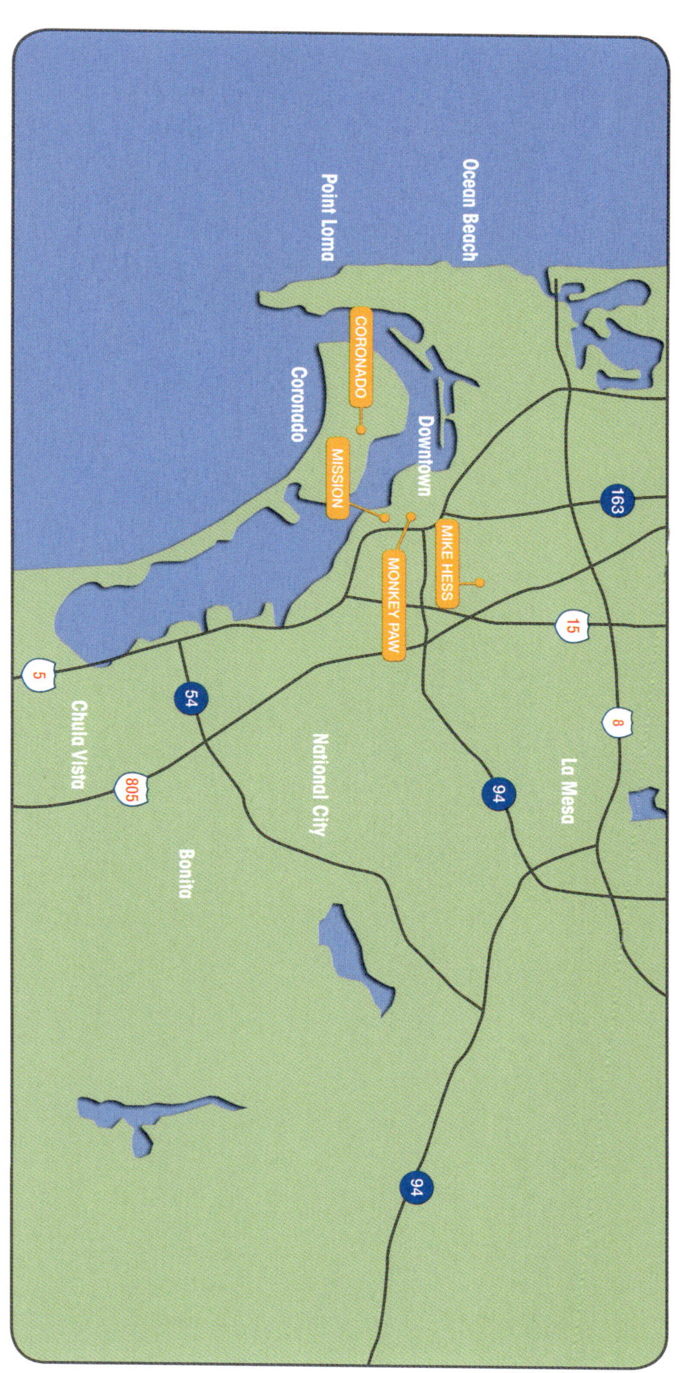
Ocean Beach
Point Loma
Coronado
CORONADO
MISSION
Downtown
MIKE HESS
MONKEY PAW
163
15
5
54
8
94
805
La Mesa
National City
Chula Vista
Bonita
94

BRETT SETTERS SECTOR 1

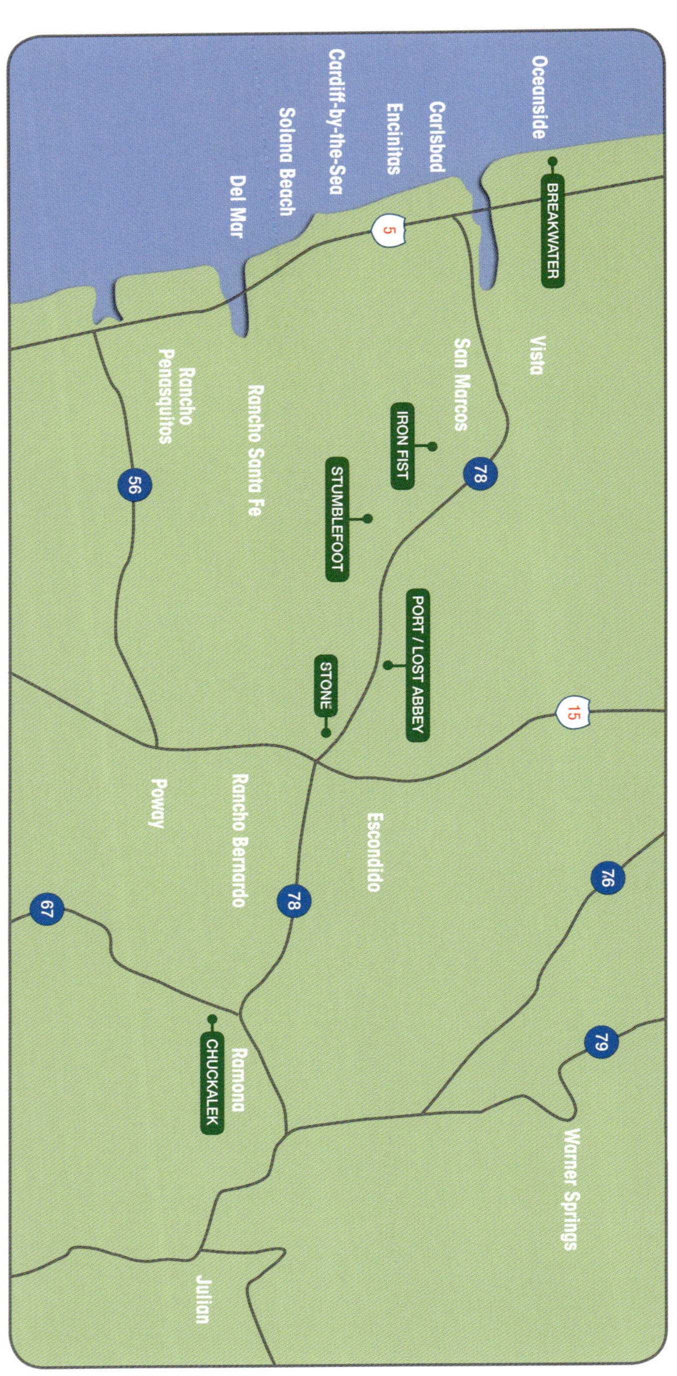

BRETT SETTERS SECTOR 2

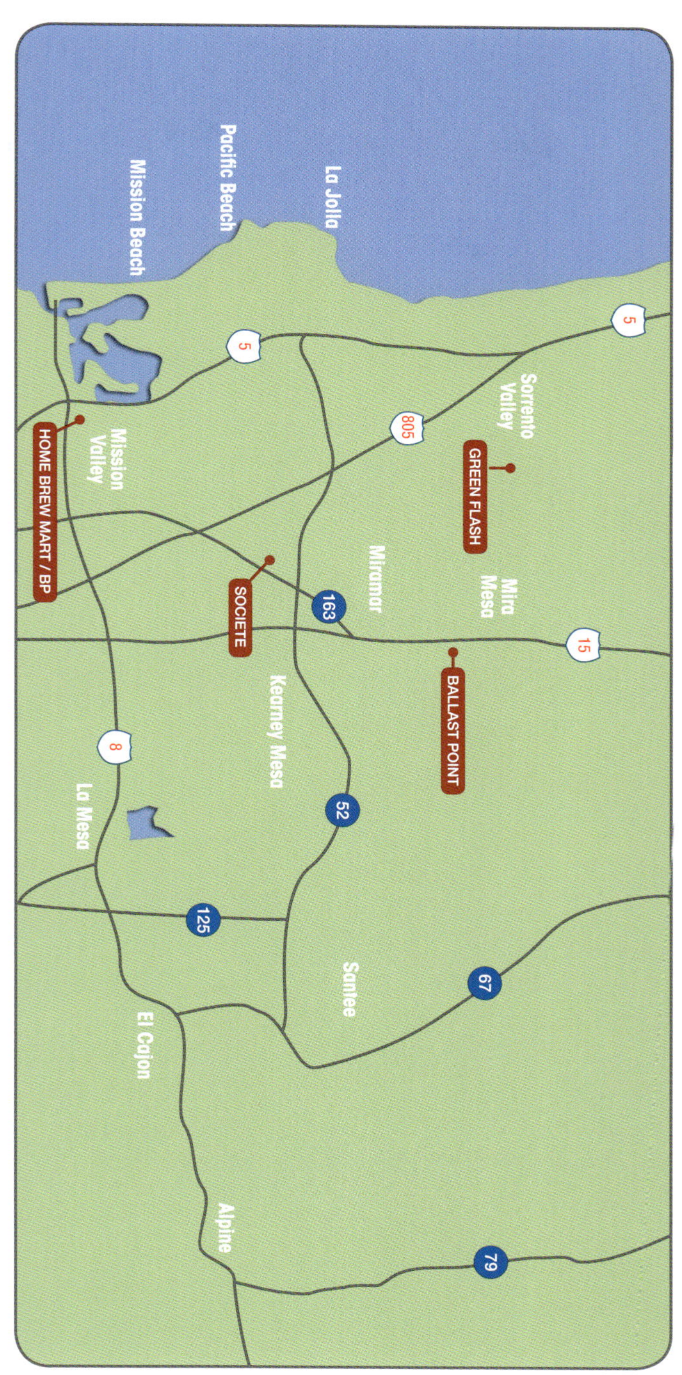

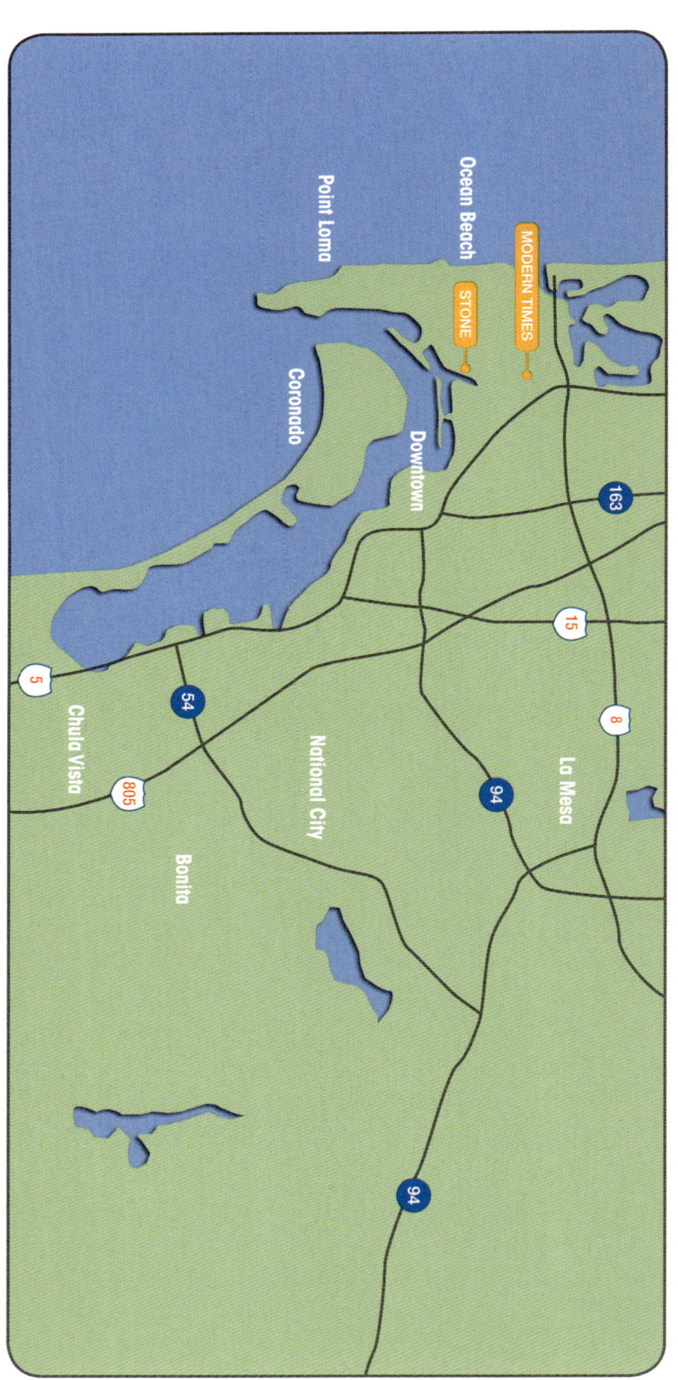
Point Loma
Ocean Beach
MODERN TIMES
STONE
Coronado
Downtown
163
15
5
8
54
Chula Vista
805
National City
94
La Mesa
Bonita
94

RED HEADS SECTOR 1

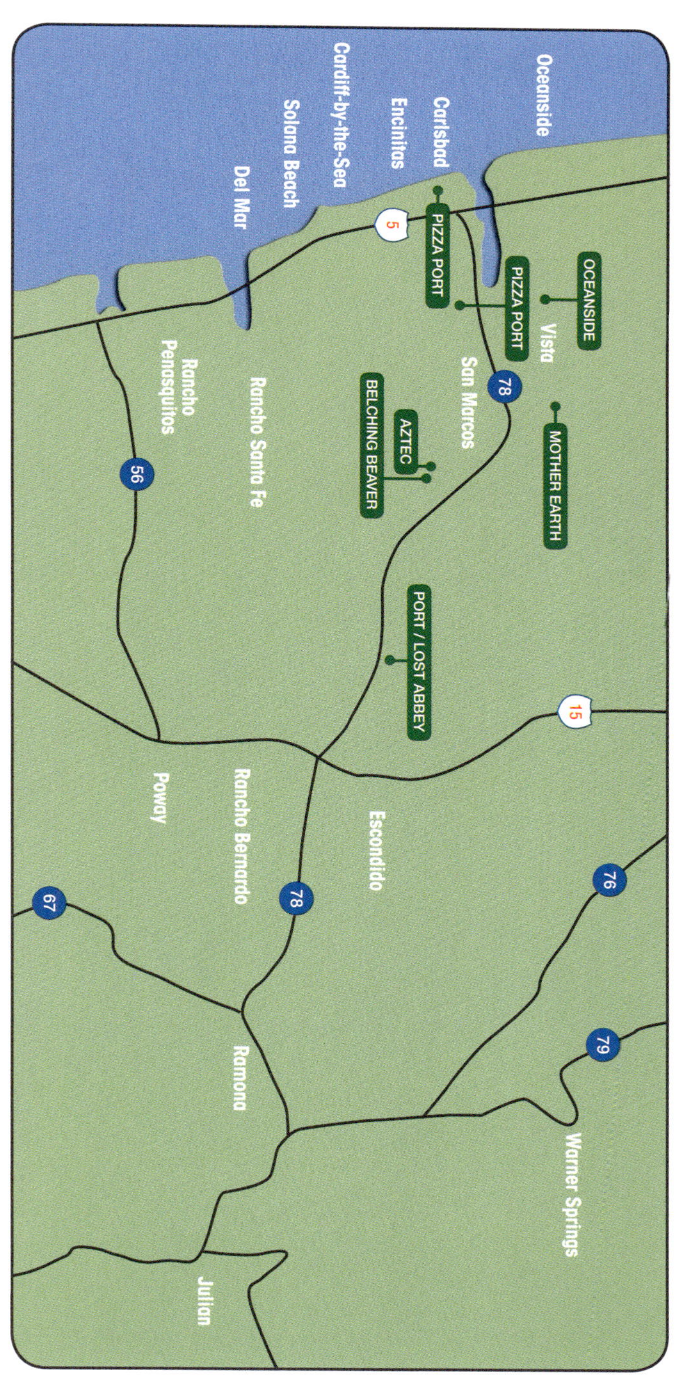

RED HEADS SECTOR 2

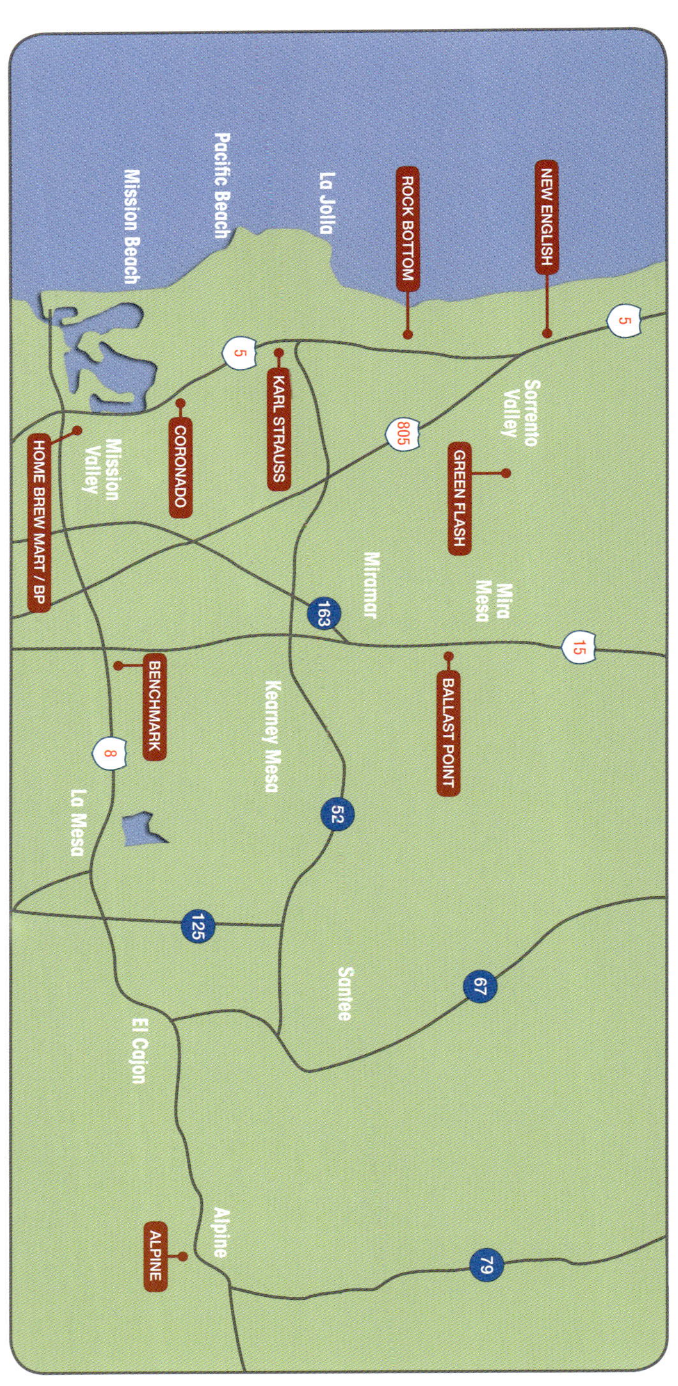

RED HEADS SECTOR 3

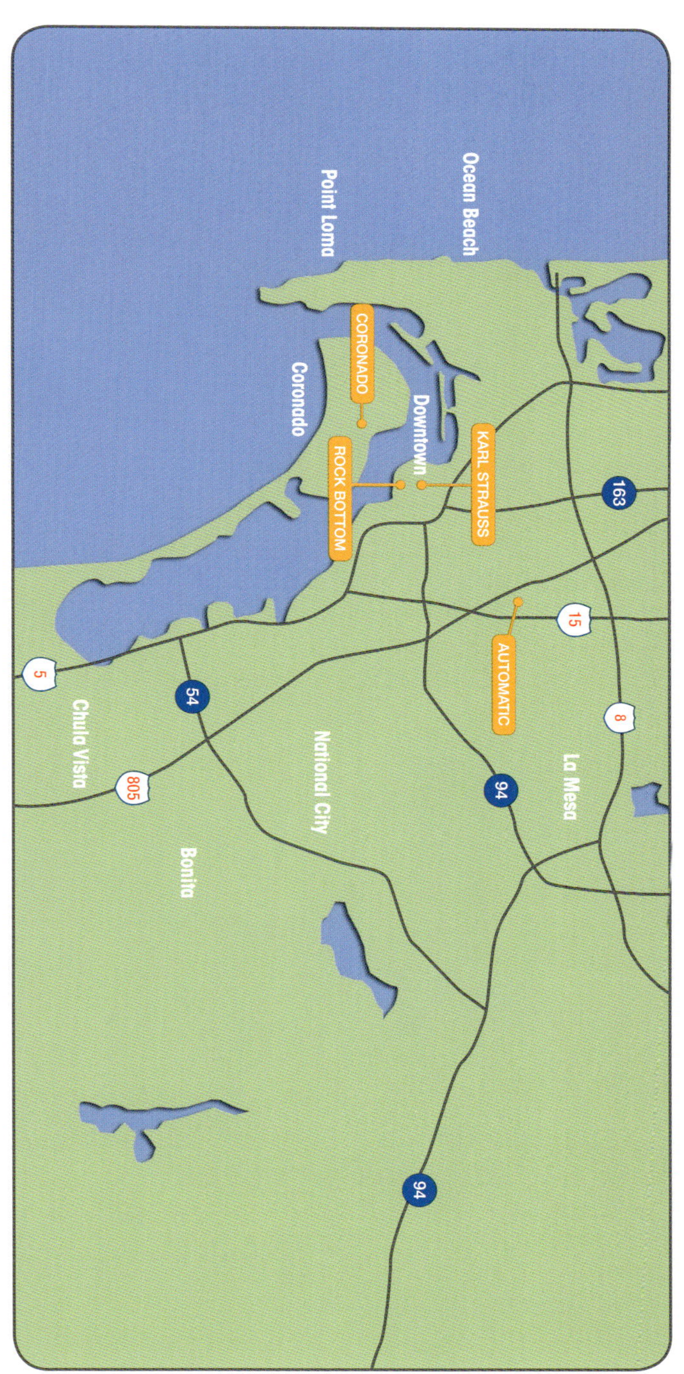

RESOURCES

GREAT BOTTLE SHOPS

Bacchus Wine Market 3
647 G St., San Diego, CA 92101
(619) 236-0005

Best Damn Beer Shop 3
Super Jr. Market, 1036 7th Ave., San Diego, CA 92101
(619) 232-6367

Beverages 4 Less 2
9181 Mission Gorge Rd., Santee, CA 92071
Phone:(619) 448-3773

Bottlecraft 3
2161 India St., San Diego, CA 92101
(619) 487-9493

Brother's Provisions 1
16451 Bernardo Center Dr., San Diego, CA 92127
(855) 850-2767

Distiller's Outlet 1
12329 Poway Rd., Poway, CA 92064
(858) 748-4617

Fletcher Hills Bottle Shop 2
2447 Fletcher Pkwy., El Cajon, CA 92020
(619) 469-8410

Holiday Wine Cellar 1
302 W. Mission Ave., Escondido, CA 92025
(760) 745-1200

KnB 2
6380 Del Cerro Blvd., San Diego, CA 92120
(619) 286-0321

Mesa Liquor & Wine Company 2
4919 Convoy St., San Diego, CA 92111
(858) 279-5292

Olive Tree Marketplace 3
4805 Narragansett Ave., San Diego, CA 92107
(619) 224-0443

Pizza Port Bottle Shop 1
571 Carlsbad Village Dr., Carlsbad, CA 92008
(760) 720-7007

Royal Liquor 1
1496 N. Coast Hwy. 101, Encinitas, CA 92024
(760) 753-4534

GREAT CRAFT BEER BARS, PUBS, AND TAVERNS

Blind Lady Ale House 3
3416 Adams Ave., San Diego, CA 92116
(619) 255-2491

Callahan's Pub and Brewery 2
8111 Mira Mesa Blvd., San Diego, CA 92126
(858) 578-7892

Churchill's Pub and Grille 1
887 W. San Marcos Blvd., San Marcos, CA 92069
(760) 471-8773

Hamilton's Tavern 3
1521 30th St., San Diego, CA 92102
(619) 238-5460

High Dive Bar & Grill 2
1801 Morena Blvd., San Diego, CA 92110
(619) 275-0460

Live Wire Bar 3
2103 El Cajon Blvd., San Diego, CA 92104
(619) 291-7450

O'Brien's Pub 2
4646 Convoy St., San Diego, CA 92111
(858) 715-1745

Ritual Tavern 3
4095 30th St., San Diego, CA 92104
(619) 283-1720

SD TapRoom 3
1269 Garnet Ave., San Diego, CA 92109
(858) 274-1010

Small Bar 3
4628 Park Blvd., San Diego, CA 92116
(619) 795-7998

Tiger! Tiger! Tavern 3
3025 El Cajon Blvd., San Diego, CA 92104
(619) 487-0401

Toronado San Diego 3
4026 30th St., San Diego, CA 92104
(619) 282-0456

Urge American Gastropub 1
16761 Bernardo Center Dr., San Diego, CA 92128
(858) 673-8743

BEER TOURS

Brewery Tours of San Diego
www.brewerytoursofsandiego.com
(619) 961-7999

Brew Hop
www.brewhop.com
(858) 361-8457

San Diego Beer & Wine Tours
lajollawinetours.com
(858) 551-5115

SAN DIEGO BEER EVENTS

March
Mission Valley Craft Beer Festival

May
Karl Strauss Beach to Brewery Beer / Music Fest

June
International Festival of Beer at Del Mar Fair

July
Belgian Beer Party at Pizza Port Carlsbad

August
Stone Anniversary Party and Beer Festival

September
San Diego Festival of Beer

November
San Diego Brewers Guild Festival / San Diego Beer Week
Green Flash Anniversary Party

COMING SOON (You want to keep an eye on these guys)

Bagby Beer Co.
http://www.bagbybeer.com/

Nickel Beer Co.
http://nickelbeerco.com/

Urban Jungle
http://urbanjunglebrewing.com/

INDEX

PICTURE CREDITS

Page 7: Courtesy San Diego Tourism Authority
Page 9: © Mike Pawlenty / Chefs Press, Inc.
Page 11: © Bruce Glassman / Georgian Bay Books, Inc.
Photos © Mike Pawlenty / Chefs Press, Inc. on pages: 12, 13, 14, 15, 16, 17, 18, 19, 20, 21, 22, 23, 28, 29, 34, 35, 36, 37, 40, 41, 42, 43, 46, 47, 48, 49, 52, 53, 56, 57, 58, 59, 60, 61, 62, 63, 74, 75, 78, 79, 80, 81, 86, 87, 88, 89, 90, 91, 92, 93, 94, 95, 98, 99, 102, 103, 105 (top and bottom), 107, 108, 109, 112, 113, 114, 115, 116, 118, 119, 120, 121, 122, 123, 124, 125, 126, 127, 128, 129, 130, 131, 134, 135, 138, 139, 140, 141
Photos © Bruce Glassman / Georgian Bay Books, Inc.: on pages 24, 25, 26, 27, 30, 31, 32, 33, 38, 39, 44, 45, 50, 51, 54, 55, 64, 65, 66, 67, 68, 69, 70, 71, 72, 73, 76, 77, 82 (bottom), 83, 84, 85, 96, 97, 100, 101, 104, 105 (middle), 106, 110, 111, 117, 132, 133, 136, 137, 142, 143
Photo page 82 (tasting room): ©Amy Krone / www.amykrone.com